MW00569637

WORD FORGING

**A modern approach for the instruction
of written expression
for students, teachers, and parents**

by

Steven J. Dykstra

Trek Associates

≡

Published by:

PO Box 110
Palmer, MA 01069
Tel/Fax: 413 283 6645
Email: TrekAssoc@aol.com
Special offers available for group and school district sales.

First edition, July 2006
[Revised, June 2007, April 2008, and October 2008]

ISBN   0-9773058-0-5
ISBN-13   978-0-9773058-0-3

Support materials are available in
Word Forging® Companion,
a CD available from Trek Associates.

1 2 3 4 5 6 7 8 9

Clipart drawings provided by Art Explosion,
© 2004 Nora Development Corporation, Calabasas, CA.

DEDICATION

There are always many people to remember and thank when an author writes his or her first book. My thoughts go back to Mrs. Bishop, a ninth-grade English teacher in my high school who pounded the basic tenets of grammar, syntax, capitalization, and punctuation into the quivering freshmen who found themselves sentenced to a nine-month internment in her class.
Of course, as tenth graders, we loved Mrs. Bishop...

Special thanks to Carla Lemnah-Warner, who helped with the initial demonstrations of this approach with students in a suburban high school; she helped prove that the initial model of Word Forging® in fact did work.

I thank the many students with whom I have worked over the years and who have taught me more than they will ever know, as well as to their parents who have encouraged me to write this text.

I owe gratitude to my parents, who both were heavily invested in the field of education.

I appreciate the understanding of my wife, Cindi, and two children, Sam & Emily, who withstood the many hours of time I have devoted to these endeavors instead of household priorities...

I thank you all.

CONTENTS

PROLOGUE

While working as a Speech and Language Pathologist and consultant with a variety of clients for over a quarter century, your author has faced numerous challenges and obstacles. First, training in the area of Communication Disorders in the mid-1970's was different than it is today. Most of the Speech Pathology college courses in those days focused on speech disorders and their specific remediation, with language interventions emerging as a considerable growing aspect of the field. Written expression, in all of its forms, was not really considered to fall within the realm of the Speech & Language Pathologist – it was an "educational" matter. However, as the years progressed, requests became more common for diagnostic and remediation input about my students' written communication in schools. I found myself doing research of the literature, developing my own formats for diagnostics and instruction, adopting and adapting the work of others, and learning every day about more ways to help my clients learn how to become more effective and efficient writers—at all ages levels.

Some problems persisted, however. The most important of these was that the more I investigated, the more complicated the approach seemed to become. There was a constant urge to employ <u>all of the latest techniques</u> with my emerging writers. I examined writing instruction in all levels of traditional education, with targeted frameworks, rubrics, goals, and objectives growing ever more numerous and complex. I soon learned that as the process of writing instruction grew more complicated for <u>*both*</u> the instructor and the instructed, the less successful the instruction became. It seemed that neither of us, student nor teacher, could see the forest but for the trees that continuously swayed, knocked each other around, and sometimes came crashing down...

In the late 1990's, I studied and became a certified hypnotist. Some people thought this was a little "far out" for a Speech and Language Pathologist. Nothing could have been further from the truth. The marriage of the two fields was a natural evolution for me, and I experienced a type of epiphany.

This endeavor grew out of a desire to find new ways to

motivate my clients in approaches that were somewhat "out of the box." (I have always been an organized person who likes to view life in "little boxes," but when it comes to helping others change and improve their behavior, I try to look at all perspectives…) I saw all around me mounting evidence about the mind/body connection, and I figured it had to play a role in working with students with learning challenges. <u>One of the most important lessons I learned in pursuit of expertise in this area was that if I wanted my clients to succeed in some aspect of change, the process had to become easier than they thought it could be.</u> If a person thinks change is too hard, too complicated, too sudden, or too much of a stretch from how life is today, that change usually will not happen.

I am reminded of the saying by Henry Ford that I have on an engraved stone placed on my desk: "Whether you think you can or you can't, you're right!" I find this particularly true of instruction in written expression, especially on the negative side of things, so I have "tweaked" the saying a bit:

> ***Whether you think you can or***
> ***cannot write, you're right!***

More on this later…

Unfortunately, we often consider the improvement of one's writing skills to be too daunting a task; we often think producing a piece of refined writing is too big a chore. (Consider, for example, the procrastination your author experienced at times when composing this book. It was too easy for life to get in the way sometimes… I should have focused on completing one chapter at a time or detailing the one step I was interested in at the time instead of focusing on "finishing the book" in its entirety.)

For the student who has difficulty in learning how to improve his or her writing, our efforts to instruct frequently make the task too challenging. We provide too little practice, place too much emphasis on product and not enough focus on the process, or too often focus on what we do not want the student to do instead of highlighting what we want him or her to start doing better.

In short, sometimes we make the task of learning how to write just too darn complicated!

My goal was to perfect an approach to writing instruction that would be easily explainable and self-motivating. I required that results be immediate, for the sake of student self-confidence. I desired to see students eager to improve skills and succeeding in this quest *in their very first attempt.* I wanted to make the process easy enough that students at almost any school age could easily learn it, remember it, take steps to teach themselves how to use it more effectively, and later show others how to do it.

Admirable goals... but achievable?

Nothing breeds success like success. *Nothing makes one a better writer than writing better.* A teacher cannot facilitate development of a student's improved self-esteem with a lecture or a pill. The student actually has to write better, and then we need to facilitate his or her realization and reinforcement of that fact. *We often erroneously assume that students learn in elementary school most of what they need to know about writing a good sentence. This is not true. Learning how to craft a well-written sentence is a life-long skill!* The third grade student cannot be expected to construct a sentence that contains complex sentence structures and vocabulary suitable for a college essay.

Why did I use the "word forging" image? I tried to visualize a process by which a writer creates a sentence and then "works" it a bit, editing and improving it slowly. This method is much like a blacksmith who "works" a piece of metal, heating it and then shaping and reshaping it until it takes on the form she or he desires. The blacksmith may have in mind the final product before starting the project, or the piece may take on a shape of its own as the creative process evolves. At each step, however, the work will grow more mature, more ornate, more detailed, and more beautiful as it is forged. The parallel to the craft of writing well was obvious to me.

This text is written primarily for the educator or Speech & Language Pathologist in mind... but through explanation of the basic format of Word Forging®, use of examples and demonstrations, and a healthy dose of anecdotal information, I hope that a wide audience will find it useful. It is my hope especially that parents gain some insight into useful aspects of this approach. I trust you will be pleased with the results.

Word Forging® is not a book that will address all of the parameters involved in teaching written expression. Our reader will have to look elsewhere for definitive information on how best to instruct lessons on a five-paragraph essay, how to develop a thesis statement, the use of metaphors and similes, round and flat character development, developing a conflict and resolution in a story, use of literary devices, etc. However, our effort here has been to establish the fundamental approach of Word Forging®, and then we have included here as well as in the Word Forging® Companion (a supplementary text, also available from Trek Associates) some activities and materials which will provide considerable support to our approach.

However, all of these skills must evolve from the simple act of writing of a good sentence.

A house built upon a weak foundation will not last. It will not support new additions and growth of the house. Parts of the house may someday come crashing down if not properly supported and designed. If a person did not have the skill foundation to craft an interesting, appropriate sentence for the reader, then all that follows is sure to be built on a wobbly base.

This is a text that will highlight some skills, in my opinion and experience, which are needed for effective writing and editing at the sentence level. Learning the steps involved in Word Forging® does not require that every sentence composed by the learner thereafter will be written at the twelfth grade level or above. Sometimes a short sentence is exactly what a good writer needs. Having the ability, nonetheless, to "forge" a sentence to improve it is exactly what the best authors can do.

Steve Dykstra
Palmer, Massachusetts
July, 2006

I. OCKHAM'S RAZOR

For years, most educators have attempted to work in the most efficient manner possible with their students. Over time, it becomes very easy, however, to get lost in a morass of complicated and seemingly endless problems related to improvements in instructional method, resulting in lots of effort but little real help for our students. As teachers' professional (and personal) lives have become more time-pressured as they attempt to fit a growing curriculum into fewer teaching opportunities, the task has become more daunting—perhaps even impossible.

In the 1400's, a scholastic by the name of William of Ockham stated the principle *Pluritas non est ponenda sine necessitate* ('Plurality should not be posited without necessity'). Simply put, he meant that all things being equal, the simpler of two explanations is the preferred one. Earlier and later philosophers, including Galileo, held that we should always look to the simpler law or principle. Ockham, however, pursued the principle so often and employed it so sharply that his principle became known as 'Ockham's Razor'...

Today, we are reminded of the KISS principle: keep it simple, stupid!

The first time, long ago, that I heard the story of Ockham's Razor, it made perfect sense to me. More recently, this led to a crystallization of another methodology which has become a cornerstone of much of what I do with my students and clients since the 1990's, called The Triad Intervention[SM].

II. THE TRIAD INTERVENTION[SM]

It has been said that people can usually only focus on (at most) three things at a time. Consider how many times in life we are confronted with, or comforted by, sets of three (<u>triads</u>):

- ¤ of the people, by the people, for the people
- ¤ one, two, three—go!
- ¤ faith, hope & charity
- ¤ morning, noon & night
- ¤ Father, Son & Holy Ghost
- ¤ executive, legislative, judicial branches
- ¤ it's as simple as A, B, C
- ¤ mind, body, & spirit

We should use the power of three's to enhance our chances of achieving our goals.

When our lives are not going well, we begin to see our goals and objectives in a negative light. We want to lose 25 pounds. We want to make it through the day without getting another big project assigned. We would like, just once, to have nothing big planned for the weekend. We want to quit smoking. We don't want to fail another test. We want to write an essay with few or no errors. We begin to see life's events as something we do not want to be or have. Instead, we should put energy into changing our lives, in positive directions, so that we can be more than we are now...

We need better definition of our goals and objectives.

Far too often, in employment evaluations, in school special education planning meetings, or in simple self-reflection in our daily lives, we spend inordinate amounts of time focusing on what people <u>cannot</u> do. (For proof of this, merely examine some Individual Educational Plans written for students with learning differences. The process is changing for the better, but older IEP's contained pages and pages about what weaknesses the child had or what the student could not do well. The plans then focused on what the child could not do… No wonder students did not want to crawl out of bed in the morning to go to school – everyone wanted them to focus on their failures!)

We become caught up in the "'yea, but…'" dilemma, continually bringing up new roadblocks in our lives, to the point of adopting learned helplessness as a way of living. We become far too tuned into our weaknesses, failures, and self-doubt. We lose our way. We do not know what our responsibilities really are. We are confused about what we should do now, next, or tomorrow morning to solve our own problems. We do not know how to succeed. (For your author, this is the <u>perfect</u> description of many students we have met who have had to struggle with learning differences in schools.)

We need better delineation of our responsibilities and immediate action steps, so that we can focus in positive directions toward change that actually helps us.

We use too much negative self-talk which drains our energies and weakens our resolve. We begin to expect failure. The foundation of our lives, which should be deeply held positive feelings of relaxation and inner balance (homeostasis), begins to be a crumbling wall of procrastination, frustration, and self-defeatism. We lose touch with our true desires. We have the anticipation of failure.

In the spring of 2002, your author was in a classroom of a mid-sized elementary school. From the room next door, he overheard the teacher telling the students that if they did not behave and be quiet before lunch, they were surely going to fail their MCAS tests (major, statewide standardized tests) next week. It was a fairly solid conclusion that some students would have trouble sitting in their seats and behaving as the teacher expected, so the adult was setting the stage for those students to do poorly on their major tests in a few days. The students were being set up to fail…

We often don't even know how to summon the expectancy of success. As therapists or teachers, we often do not know how to help our clients establish a truly "safe place" in their lives, let alone help them to succeed in a task. We merely assume that getting an "A" on a paper or project will make all students feel good! Far too often, the student does not really know why he or she earned the grade that was received—good or bad.

We need to re-establish the balance in our experiences, the sense of relaxation that comes with being 'okay' with our lives, and the use of proper stress management techniques.

Our work with children and adults since 1978 at Trek Associates has gradually perfected an approach which is simple, positively focused, and which facilitates our client's own identification of solutions to their presenting issues. Building on the desire to use at most three elements, the Triad Intervention[SM] (as we have called it) is based on the analysis of three elements:

1] Clarification of reasonable positive goals & objectives
2] Determining responsibilities & action steps that the client must do
3] Employing relaxation, promoting the learning of proper stress management techniques and achieving balance in life

We have chosen the symbol of a triangle in our Trek Associates business logo:

We also have chosen the triangle as part of the pictorial representation of the Triad Intervention[SM] process:

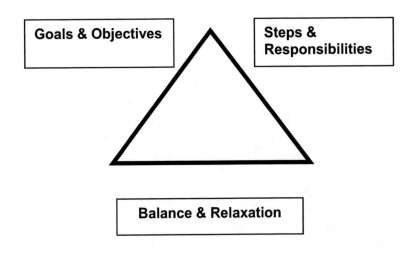

© 2001, Trek Associates

This process seems amazingly simple. For some, it appears too simple. However, we have rarely helped our clients achieve real change in their lives unless this process was implemented.

In the helping professions, we owe it to our clients to help them reach understanding of their issues and challenges, closure on what to do about them, and the sense of peace that comes with having a plan that works. Interestingly, the client often has a commendable ability to identify important aspects of his or her own needs. It is our job to help the person clarify what needs focus right now. The process is dynamic. It may point to focusing first on an internal balance. Once that is achieved, new goals and objectives may arise. Then we may need to refocus on steps and responsibilities. At any static point in time, however, The Triad Intervention[SM] analysis helps to clarify. When we see our near future in a clearer, sharper, more focused manner, we tend to feel better. We also tend to succeed, or at least feel that we are moving in the right direction. A plan can always be "tweaked."

The issues detailed above focus on clinical and therapeutic

parameters. However, experience as a Speech and Language clinician working with school-aged children suggests that the very same issues often apply to the teaching of writing skills. *Amazingly, the process described above also seems uniquely suited to the instruction of written expression!*

We need better definition of those goals and objectives we expect our students to aim for when learning to write. We need to explain in better terms our students' responsibilities and the immediate action steps we wish them to take. Yes, some students will "just learn" to write like a duck takes to water; their facility for language development (oral or written) seems to require no outside, prescribed intervention. It is a natural development for them.

For many other students, however, the truth of the matter is that they will become better writers only once we, their teachers, do a better job of teaching them.

As stated previously, we far too often make the process too complicated. Sometimes we "teach" (= introduce) a skill and then provide far too few opportunities to practice that skill. For still some other students, those with specific learning differences and/or written expression challenges, merely showing the student what to do when engaging in a writing lesson is not enough. This type of person will not just "pick it up." He or she must be shown, in discrete steps and through specific processes, what is expected. He or she must have frequent and repeated opportunities to succeed at the process. The skill needs to be discretely taught and then automatized, sometimes in very small steps. You cannot take a pill to become a good writer.

When teachers, parents, and other adults provide too many steps, make the leaps in learning too wide, or help the student achieve one success and then assume he or she "knows" how to write, a grave mistake is made. We need to focus on what students can do (not on their mistakes in writing), helping them to continually shape and expand their writing skills. We need to give them goals to aim towards, not away from. We need to instill the sense of responsibility for writing improvement clearly in the student. If we too easily accept a deficient assignment that is turned in, correct and edit it for the student, and then ask for a final rewritten copy, then we have not worked cooperatively with the student to write the paper or essay. Only when we explain what we want a student to do and then give full responsibility for reaching that goal to the student can s/he begin to develop the ultimate goals — an improved self–confidence and a demonstrated skill in written expression.

The teacher can create a scenario in which the student begins a process of improved and independent task completion. When a student can improve his or her work as compared to previous attempts and make adjustments which are needed, then the seeds of true, independent learning have been planted.

Moreover, if we make a "plan for instruction" which is too ambitious, too complicated, or too unfamiliar, it is doomed to fail. (OK, let's see how long we can keep this student's IEP a secret from him...) Experience as a clinician and therapist has shown repeatedly that when one sets out a plan with many steps, we hope that we have been comprehensive in complete in formulating what needs to happen for success. We can establish a great plan with seventeen steps that seems to "guarantee" that the end goal will be reached. However, in the mind of the client or student, if just one step of that seventeen-step plan fails, the plan itself begins to crumble. If the person works hard but cannot remember or cannot achieve one of the necessary steps of the plan, then there is the temptation to say, "It just doesn't work."

The need for simplicity, unfortunately, is actually difficult for some professionals to accept or to understand.

Years (even careers) have been spent in the development of comprehensive, extensive, and somewhat complicated approaches to the teaching of writing, and yet we still see students and adults who cannot write reasonably well. They do not have the tools to monitor and improve their own work in specific ways.

When the teacher returns a manuscript and says, "That is a good try, but now make it better," these students are lost—they do not know what to do next. When a teacher tells them what is not good about the paragraph, essay, or paper, these students may understand what they <u>should not do</u>, but they are clueless about what they <u>should do</u> to improve their work. You would be surprised (or maybe you would not be surprised...) at how often this actually happens in a modern high school. We have seen it frequently in <u>every</u> school in which we have worked.

There is a proverb about the relative value of giving a hungry person some food for today or teaching him/her to grow food for tomorrow—which is better? We can make the analogy work for the teaching of writing. We can give a student the assistance to help him or her finish a given assignment (to earn today's grade in the grade book) or we can teach him or her the skills necessary to write, edit, and improve writing abilities tomorrow and every day thereafter.

Use of the Triad Intervention[SM] enables us to look at this issue very simply. Our own work has shown, time and time again, that real change can occur in habit control, skill development, and life orientations when we look at three aspects:

- ✓ The goal, which in this case is to become a better writer
- ✓ The steps and responsibilities which the student must learn and develop (mastery of some core skills)
- ✓ The sense of balance, understanding, and acceptance that the development of new writing skills and achievement will bring to the life of the student

Put another way, if the student does not know what the goal of writing instruction truly is, if she or he does not understand or cannot use the prerequisite skills necessary to get there, and if she or he does not really care about the writing task or does not see why it is important to complete the process, then little hope of success will be observed in writing instruction.

Some people will say it cannot be as simple as that... We maintain that to make it any more complicated than that will only result in failure.

Students generally do want to write well, at least well enough to meet teacher expectations. When a teacher fails to make expectations clear, however, then problems occur. In the Triad Intervention[SM] model, this equates to a person's not being clear about the goal. If you do not know where you are going or what you are aiming for, you will have a challenge.

Far too often, we have observed teachers who do not explain why they are asking students to do a specific task. (For some clear proof of this, how many students currently in special education truly know and understand the learning goals which a team of professionals have established in their Individual Education Plans? How many students actually play an <u>active role</u> in developing their own IEP's? Many students do not attend their own meetings.) Your author has counseled many students who received a poor grade on a paper or assignment, not because of shoddy or incomplete effort by the student but because of unclear directions by the teacher. The students were confused about the assignment. We have been confused ourselves by the instructions that some teachers have provided to their students for the completion of a classroom writing task.

Perhaps worse yet, we have observed the poor writing skills demonstrated by some teachers, invoking the "do as I say, not as I do" message to their students. Clearly, some students do not see any value at all in completing a given writing assignment, or in learning to write a 5-paragraph essay, or in revealing their indifference in opinion essays. How rewarding can a writing assignment be when the teacher collects papers and then takes days or even weeks to return the work? (Often, such papers have only a general grade, simplistic feedback comments, or the infamous "check mark" provided as an evaluation of student effort and achievement in completing the assignment.) Surprisingly, some teachers may <u>never</u> return a given assignment to students, reinforcing an impression that the task was just "busy work" in the first place or that the grade was the focus, not the learning opportunities of the writing process itself.

If we want to help many of our students make solid and specific gains in writing, we need to provide them with a clear goal for the instructional task, delineate specific steps we want them to employ, and we need to motivate them properly or give them some assurance of the potential to achieve a valued reward. The number of steps should be limited and concrete (achievable), not too numerous and complicated. If we can make the reward for task completion an internal reinforcement that works for the individual, then we truly are focusing on steps that promote learning.

Let us pause for a second and consider the contention that many people HATE the processes of reviewing, revising, and rewriting what they have written. There is a real preference demonstrated by many high school students today to sit down, handwrite a paragraph or essay to complete an assignment, and then submit the work. No proofreading or revisions... (Why? Perhaps because the student knows his or her teacher will make necessary corrections before a final draft is required... Let the teacher do the work!) We need to convince the student that revision is part of the process, a needed step. It can be, in fact, the real fun part of writing. As Sol Stein says, "The biggest difference between a writer and a would-be writer is their attitude toward rewriting. The writer, professional or not, looks forward to the *opportunity* of excising words, sentences, paragraphs, chapters that do not work and to improving those that do. Many a would-be writer thinks whatever he puts down on paper is by that act somehow indelible... Unwillingness to revise usually signals an amateur" (Stein, 1995, p. 277).

If I could show you a way of teaching writing skills so that the student has a clear goal, just three steps to use, and a way for him or her to challenge him/herself to improve, would it make sense to use it?

Yes – I think it would.

If I could show you a way to change a student's orientation from "I can't" to "I can," would it help to promote more confidence in writing skills?

Yes, we can anticipate that it would.

After just a few minutes of instruction, we have observed classrooms full of "poor writers" jump to their computers, eager to be the first one in the group to reach the writing goal we have set for them. We have also observed students in those classrooms reach the goal before the end of the class period. We have observed smiles and even some fist pumps ("YES!!!!") as these students succeed in the steps we have given them. We have shown them that they can do it!

Would it be useful for the classroom teacher to be able to tell a student at what grade level he or she is writing, not for evaluation purposes but as a signpost of progress and as a motivator? Would a high school senior find value in writing a college application essay that actually is composed at the high school level? Would a student love to write some sentences that are above his or her grade level?

Yes, we believe so.

Welcome to Word Forging®.

III. EFFECTIVE INSTRUCTION

A fair number of teachers will look at the methods we are proposing and respond, "I've been teaching for thirty-five years, and I think I know how to teach – the old fashion way is best: have a student sit down with a pencil and write!"

Historical reference to the development of writing is relevant to our discussion of effective instruction. Sue Tomlinson (1998b) provides a useful brief history of written expression starting from early man. One of the reasons we know so little about early man (or woman) is that he (or she) did not write anything down! Early cultures were at the mercy of natural forces. Early civilizations tended to act out their stories or references to nature, passing down stories and information from one generation to the next. The first attempt to actually record information may have been in the form of naturalistic paintings of animals and people. Over time, these drawings and paintings became stylized and perhaps more abstract.

In Egypt, these representational symbols evolved into what we today call hieroglyphics. The Native Americans of the Southwest painted figures, which we now call petroglyphs, in cliffs and caves to represent information along trade routes, ritual information, and many other things. The different tribes did not always speak the same language, but their written symbols were quite similar and were understood by travelers. In the ancient times of Europe, runes (pictorial figures) or oghams (a system of alphabet writing) were used. The Romans spread their written language as they conquered various parts of the world.

Where a written language was not adopted and peoples depended only on verbal memories or histories, much of their culture has been lost to us. The peoples of the Far East, including the Chinese, used a pictorial writing that represented a visual depiction of an idea, but over the years these visualizations became more stylized and abstract. Poetry in some languages, like Chinese and Japanese, is mostly visual while in others, such as English, it is mostly oral.

Finally, about 3500 years ago, the Phoenicians first derived a written alphabet that represented sounds, not pictures or ideas. A set of 20 to 40 sound symbols represent the major sounds in many languages. Eventually, the written language of the Phoenicians spread throughout the Middle East and was adapted by the Arabs and Greeks. The Greek variations further evolved into the Cyrillic alphabets of countries like Russia, and the Romans developed the Roman alphabet. The Roman alphabet is used by many countries in the Americas and Europe today. More recently, some aspects of the written Japanese and Chinese languages have been developed which employ the sounds of the language rather than a pictorial image of an idea. This has resulted in faster typing and word processing in those languages. As Sue Tomlinson says, however, "the art form of Chinese and Japanese writing will very likely never die" (Tomlinson, 1998b).

Stone was the first writing surface, followed by papyrus (layers of reed), vellum and parchment (animal skins), old cloth fibers (paper), and finally wood fibers (paper). The invention of the printing press by Johannes Gutenberg set the stage for the rapid transmission of the printed word throughout the world. This event is considered by many to be one of the most important happenings in the history of the world, certainly the intellectual world.

Prior to the development of the printing press, books such as the Bible had to be copied by hand. In Ireland, the Celts followed the teachings of St. Patrick and became noted scholars. They learned to perform some of the most beautiful manuscript writing in the ancient world, but these scribes also developed short cuts. In the old world, all letters in manuscripts were capitals. The Irish scribes gradually reduced the size of letters in the body of a manuscript to speed the process of copying; these new sized letters became our small letters. Monks in monasteries all over the world took on the task of laboriously copying new editions of the Bible, sometimes with amazing calligraphy and artwork. It might take a year or more to copy a large book. Due to the spread of the Catholic religion and other reasons, the art of writing spread throughout many parts of the world.   In other cultures, religious documents such as the Torah or the Koran were also copied and handed down from generation to generation.

Tomlinson (1998b) notes that writing was not universally welcomed as it developed over time. Plato, the famous Greek philosopher, felt that written language would lead to the destruction of memory in people. Ancient Greeks could memorize tens of thousands of lines of poetry after only a few exposures to them. That ability rarely continues today. Secondly, he believed that writing ideas down could easily lead to misunderstandings. Eventually, mankind has accepted these shortcomings and has learned to appreciate the history that a written language affords us. We have the energy we can spend on higher order reasoning when we do not have to remember so many details. We gain the ability to experience knowledge and learning that is cumulative over history, broadening of social democracies that allow more knowledge and information to reach the masses. We even have the ability to build on information in order to create new technologies in less than a generation (Tomlinson, 1998b).

Our experiences with Early Intervention have taught us some important lessons. EI programs attempt to identify youngsters, from age 0—3 years, who have developmental, cognitive, learning, or physical challenges. Individualized programs are then developed to address the needs of the child and to work with family members to promote the optimal supportive environment. The Speech and Language Pathologist in this setting works with family members and other professionals to promote the development of receptive and expressive language as well as interdisciplinary efforts for other skills.

How does this relate to the instruction of writing? Of course, the SLP does not work on specific writing skills at this level, but certainly the precursors for a multitude of prewriting skills are addressed. A more fundamental element is at play here, however.

Some children take to language development as a duck takes to water. It comes "naturally," often through observation, interaction, verbal play, experimentation, shaping over time, and reinforcement. From the moment a child begins to associate something that sounds like "momma" with security and food to the epiphany that comes when she or he discovers the value of "no!" at the age of two, some youngsters just naturally absorb language like a sponge. Others, not necessarily unfortunately but just because they learn differently, must learn language skills through more direct, discrete instruction. The parents (and eventually teachers or other professionals) must provide specific opportunities for review and feedback. Eventually, as children develop more confidence and success in their language skills, they begin to expand their language without such formalized interventions. This process, however, may have to be repeated when they begin learning any new realm of skills—in the gymnasium, in music class, in social interactions with friends and adults, in a new job, in reading and spelling, and of course in writing.

The tasks of learning change over time. One of the best explanations and depictions of this fact has been done in the work of Dr. Mel Levine. For example, in grades one through three, there is a surge in the demand for phonological memory used in reading, writing, and spelling and an initial integration of language in writing skills. In grades nine through twelve, there is a growing stress on abstract and figurative language and an increased linguistic-ideational density in texts. Word processing skill becomes a crucial need in high school. We highly recommend that the reader consult Dr. Levine's "Neurodevelopmental Themes Over Time: Some Evolving School-Related Expectations" (Levine, et al., 2000). Dr. Levine also talks about writing deficits as a developmental output failure (see the AllKindsofMinds.com website for a great resource about this material).

As Sue Tomlinson notes in "Some Facts About Language" (Tomlinson, 1998d), Noam Chomsky estimated that they may be 500,000 descriptive rules of a language (word order, pronunciation, word formation, and sentence structure). Most people learn their native language by experimentation and imitation. English spelling rules seem extremely difficult, but these rules have not changed appreciably in the past 250 years. The English speaker can generally learn most of the 235 important rules by reading often. Attempting to learn them explicitly, as in structured instruction, can be a real challenge.

Research has demonstrated often that the skill of reading is how most people learn to write grammatically correct sentences.

When we read our language, we pick up on how it is used in its rich complexity.

Specifically in the development of writing skills, some people require direct, explicit instruction. These individuals have difficulty just "picking it up naturally." Then, guided practice is a necessity, with frequent and (hopefully) immediate feedback. Lastly, they need opportunities for independent practice of their new skill. Especially in writing skills, the assumption that a skill is "once taught, once learned" can be particularly erroneous.

However, as any professional author or editor will attest, the statements above pertain not only to those young students who "learn differently." Considerable effort and time are devoted to painstakingly improving a novel or newspaper article. Doctorate degrees are made or broken on the language expressed in the Ph.D. dissertation. International incidents can result from the use of the wrong word by a Head of State. In today's world, the use of the computer's word processor has simplified the processes of writing, correcting, editing, and revising one's writing.

Your author was the first person to own a personal computer at the private school where he worked in the 1980's. I can remember vividly pondering that purchase in the business machine store which sold the new computer equipment. The salesman said that owning such a device would create all types of free time in my workday. Later, the business world would embrace the computer because it would allow the company with the latest and most powerful data processing to stay ahead of the competition. At the time, we anticipated the computerized life would leave us all types of time to devote to the more important things in life.

We were wrong.

Computers did not leave us with considerably more free time. In fact, just the opposite happened for many people. The ability to have the latest information or the fastest "crunched" data led to a never-ending spiral of need for more information, all the time. The exploding capabilities of the Internet and the World Wide Web encouraged us to search for more information, and then more, and then more again.

Since 1995, for example, the amount of disk space used to store personal information on individuals has absolutely skyrocketed (Sweeney, 2002). It used to be that what people needed to know on a daily basis related to food and survival. It was rare that a person would travel more than seven miles from home during a lifetime. News did not travel quickly. Then, in the mid-1400's, Gutenberg developed the first printing press, and information began to travel faster. People expanded their knowledge base beyond their daily survival. News traveled farther and faster. The invention of the computer allowed news to travel at lightning speed, and we can store and seek immense amount of information far removed from our daily survival needs. Today, the needs to have information available and to communicate it efficiently and effectively are essential to our society. As Blas Pedro Uberuaga states, "information has become the backbone of our society" (Uberuaga, 1993). It has also been said that one edition of the Sunday "New York Times" contains more information than the average person in the Middle Ages needed to learn in their entire lifetime!

I can remember telling an associate that the real value of the internet would become the sharing of information world wide, and I even stated that one great use of the WWW might be auctions—present information and even pictures of items you have to sell, and then offer them to the highest bidder. My associate said it would never work; "people want to touch or closely examine things they want to buy at an auction, so it will never work."

That was five years before today's popular Internet auction websites arrived on the scene…

One of the problems, many people say, of encouraging students to learn to use a computer or a word processor in the development of their writing skills is that the task quickly becomes too complicated, to extensive, too overwhelming—unless we tweak the method a bit.

Almost twenty years ago, research was demonstrating that

most teachers focused on the final product of writing but had little understanding of the process used by a writer to create that product (Hansen, 1987). Students often wrote their essays but had little interest in learning the skills to tweak their compositions; most of the attention was given to content, the message, and most were afraid of confronting those thousands of rules that were required to produce a truly correct composition in all linguistic and grammatical aspects. Any enthusiasm that a person might have for the ideas in the essay might be squashed when it came to actually doing the writing.

The arrival of that personal computer with its word processing capabilities should have been considered a watershed event in the instruction of writing skills in our schools. As a teacher in the 1980's, I should have foreseen the ability of the personal computer to encourage students to record their ideas, organize and make their message tighter, and then edit the construction so that the final product could be a true work of art. As Marjorie Simic states in her article, "Computer Assisted Writing Instruction," a teacher must always be aware that integrating advanced technology into the a curriculum does not eliminate problems. However, "as a tool for practice in writing, the word processor's usefulness is unparalleled. Writing researchers have long advised that the key to fluent writing it to write as much as possible. The key to exact writing is to revise repeatedly" (Simic, 1994). Ms. Simic contends that prior to the microcomputer, an instructional model of writing was not often employed because writing, rewriting, correcting and retyping just took too much time. Students, and sometimes their teachers, did not always think that the benefits of the revision process were worth the mechanics of repeated rewriting (Simic, 1994).

Your present author was a fairly competent typist in college, and therefore he was asked by many of his friends and classmates to type their papers for a small fee. The arrival of error correction technologies on some of the IBM Selectric typewriters was a real relief. In fact, nothing was more frustrating than completing a bibliography, with all of its entries written page after page in alphabetical order based on the authors' last names, and then discovering that you mistakenly had omitted one book beginning with a B and another beginning with a K. This usually meant having to redo the entire bibliography. Try doing this sometime on a manual typewriter (if you can find one), and you will quickly get the point...

Merely using a word processor does not guarantee improved writing skills, however. MacArthur and Graham (1987) reported no differences in the number and type of revisions learning disabled students made using paper and pencil methods versus word processing. Final drafts of the two groups of writers did not significantly differ. Nonetheless, instruction in how to do revisions effectively in combination with word processing did improve significantly the amount and quality of revisions by learning disabled students (Graham and McArthur, 1988). For many students, typing is considerably easier than handwriting, and it produces a neater, more visually pleasing end product (MacArthur, et al, 1993).

Research and development of better interventions continue, but the focus needs to be on fine-tuning the use of technology based on effectiveness. As Charles MacArthur notes, "The challenge for special educators is two-fold: First, existing research on word processing makes it clear that simply providing technology to teachers and students will not result in improvements in student writing. Effective instructional methods must be developed that make use of the power provided by these tools to enhance the writing of students with LD. Second... *researchers need to go beyond word processing to investigate the effects of instruction using a wide range of technological tools to support writing*" (MacArthur, 1996, emphasis added).

There are a number of reasons why students may display poor handwriting. The child may have been criticized early in life for poor drawing skills; he could not color "between the lines" well enough to satisfy a teacher or parent. Students may not get enough practice in handwriting, or television and computer games may interfere with their writing time. The student may never have been rewarded with anything of value (to him or her) for displaying nice handwriting. The Accelerated Schools in Denver, Colorado, present a website (Write555.com) which has as its goal to stop handwriting problems – quick! Early intervention programs can encourage young children (aged 2) to draw straight lines. Kids at age 3 can have fun with zig zag lines and tracing from left to right. Older children, up to age 5, can begin to print some letters. In the 21st Century, however, there is a skill that cannot be neglected.

Educators today who are not fully implementing a word processing approach to the teaching of writing may be missing a

great opportunity. However, many of the teachers who are instructing our young learners today in fact were themselves taught to write <u>without</u> word processors, so they perhaps are not familiar with some innovative techniques.

More recent college graduates with majors in education may or may not have great writing skills themselves. One of the significant complaints of college professors today is the lack of competent writing skills of their incoming freshmen. The majority of colleges in 2006 have begun to offer assistance to all their students through campus Writing Labs or Learning Centers. Many colleges now have writing-across-the-curriculum policies that mandate that professors require students to employ effective writing skills in all of their classes. We still need to do some catching up...

William DuBay (DuBay, undated) writes about the "Price of Poor Writing." He suggests that many highly paid workers spend up to 85% of their daily work time in writing tasks. He notes that computer manufacturer Coleco lost $35 million, and eventually went out of business, when customers could not decipher the instruction manuals for the Adam line of computers and rushed to return their purchases for refund. Example after example can be provided to show how businesses and organizations lose time and money because of poor writing. Justin Pope (Pope, 2005) indicated that two-thirds of companies surveyed for a 2004 report said that writing was an important skill for employees; 75% of the companies said they considered writing abilities when hiring new employees. The College Board's National Commission on Writing reported that more than 40% of responding companies offered or required training in writing skills for their salaried employees with writing deficiencies. Writing was considered a "marker" attribute of high-wage work, a "gatekeeper" for higher salaries. "Writing skills cannot be developed quickly or easily, but should be the focus of school and college attention across the curriculum, from kindergarten through college" (College Board, 2005B). The National Commission on Writing further reported that the annual cost of training current state employees as a group was $221 million dollars, excluding hospital, educational, and local employees (College Board, 2005A).

In 2002, Columbia University completed a five-year process of evaluating and planning a revitalized undergraduate writing program. The new program focused on three premises: 1) reading and writing skills are developed at the same time, 2) one must practice writing, and it can be learned by most people even if it cannot be simplified to a set of firm rules and procedures, and 3) good writing will always be motivated by some purpose. Columbia's writing center was not planned to be a "one stop fix-it shop" where students could come by to get help on a single paper. Instead, the hope was that a student would develop a relationship with a tutor and begin to work together over the entire course of his or her undergraduate education. Here, then, we find the faculty of one of the premier college-level institutions in our country realizing that a change in focus was needed in their support of their students' written expression (Devitt, 2002).

In 2004, staff at Michigan State University developed a "Plan for Strengthening Undergraduate Writing Instruction" to meet the needs of students in the 21st Century. Additionally, the faculty wanted to underscore the importance of being a productive writer, being able to present information but also to acquire, explore, and create knowledge. A report noted that one of the foremost challenges for universities in this century would be to educate students who can participate in a global economy built upon new technologies. Writers will need to understand and to navigate the world between culture and technology. "We must all become more adept at writing with technology, writing within communities, and writing across cultures" (Porter, et al., 2004).

Staff who teach at colleges and universities are becoming increasingly aware that the demands of productivity in the 21st Century require some new strategies and skills. "In an information age, writing and the teaching of writing are increasingly technology intensive processes. The traditional values of a sound writing curriculum – teaching students to produce articulate, well-developed, supported arguments with attention to audience, purpose, and eloquence of delivery – have not changed, but writing tools have changed tremendously and will continue to change... To be successful in the global information economy, students must communicate effectively using computer technologies" (Porter, et al., 2004).

Many people fear, however, that learning how to write effectively is just too complicated – "If I did not learn how to write before high school, I will never learn to do it well!" The reality of the situation in American education today is that many teachers feel that instruction of writing skills to students in senior high school is just not their responsibility – "they should have learned how to write long before they got to me!" Therefore, it seems to make sense not to penalize students for poor grammar, spelling errors, confusing punctuation, and sentences that are not well written.

In contrast, we would love to see ALL teachers at the high school level with the same high expectations in terms of written work. Students should be able to write at their grade level, either with or without special strategies or other supports. This should be a major focus of American education, not just an afterthought or a skill for the advanced student.

Writing across the curriculum is a very important concept. Expository writing is useful in all subjects. Good writing skills improve reading comprehension skills (Tompkins, 2001). Students learn to organize, question, and revise their thoughts while reading the works of others. Yet, many teachers in high school content classes other than English feel that writing skills are not an area of focus for their instructional interventions. Many of the teachers we have observed do not correct errors in spelling, grammar, or punctuation in their students' papers.   Moreover, it begs the question: are these teachers even <u>aware</u> of these errors?

Too many teachers, in fact, have their own fears of using complicated computer software, or they have never learned to do so. In some cases, preparing students for the demands of the 21st Century may be an example of the blind leading the blind... Mark Cuban, in the "What's Next Forum" on Time Magazine (March 20, 2006) stated, "In the past, you had to memorize knowledge because there was a cost to finding it. Now, what can't you find in 30 seconds or less? We live in an open-book-test life that requires a completely different skill set." To prepare students well for the future, we need to give them the tools. Inherent in this statement is the understanding that to give students the tools they need, our teachers need to own those same tools. We need to make the process as easy for teachers as we make it for the learners.

We also need to do something else, something to address the bottom of that Triad Intervention^{SM} triangle. It is essential that we create some sense of motivation and balance in the student so that it will make sense that he or she works on writing skills. Bradley-Johnson and Lesiak (1989) cited works which suggested that teachers often create anxiety through their instructional methods – specifically, requiring students to write for a grade. In our experience, very few high school teachers encourage students to write for the mere fun of writing. That concept has been pounded out of students many years earlier. Usually, high school writing tasks are all assigned a grade. In fact, some teachers have to use the threat of a zero in the grade book to get students to do the assignment. Yup, that sure is a great way to promote the joy of writing.

We need to focus on motivation first, then process and procedure. If we do not motivate the student to do his or her best on any assignment, graded or not, we are not facilitating the expression of the student's potential. As Streur tells us, "Whether your goal is to motivate students to write prose or poetry, generating meaningful topics to develop into stories and poems is the foundation of a successful writing program" (Streur, 1999, p.78).

Remember Ockham's Razor? We need to make the

instruction of writing skills simpler than the learner thought it
could be.

You are now ready for Word Forging®.

IV. WORD FORGING^SM

Right now, before you read any further, get out a piece of paper and write a sentence about your day or your job. Keep that sentence safely until we ask for it again...

It took years for your author to formulate the following procedures. The task was not done based on a desire to "discover" some new, neat, cute way to learn to write for marketing purposes; it was based on need. People, both teachers and students, were asking for help and unsure how to get it. The core motivation to write this book in fact was derived from the encouragement of parents of students with whom we have worked. "You need to let other people know about this" was a common theme of their input.

As we have stated, our explicit model for writing sentences had some prerequisites:

1) Direct instruction capabilities, including a plan or strategy which helps students feel more comfortable with the process

2) Limited in steps (no more than 3 in the basic approach) to promote memory of the process (demystification)

3) Availability for immediate feedback and reinforcement

4) Amenable to frequent opportunities for independent practice

5) Self-motivating

6) Adaptable to a wide range of students and age levels (primary, middle school, and high school students, English as a Second Language, language impaired, etc.)

7) Serve as a platform for development of support skills (parts of speech, punctuation, grammar) or a foundation for more advanced writing skills (such as paragraph development, multi-paragraph essays, and other literary skills)

8) Promote the development of editing and proofreading skills (and reinforcing the value of these skills, which are so often avoided by school-aged writers)

9) Opportunity to incorporate easily the specific skills which are learned into other academic arenas, not just "English class," and to reinforce writing skills across the curriculum

10) Promote the learning of a life-long skill, not just a lesson that will soon become irrelevant or unneeded, because it makes so much sense to use it

Teachers, many who are effective writers themselves, participate in training workshops for improving their instruction of written expression. However, they frequently remain challenged when they attempt to try to use their "new information" with students who demonstrate learning challenges or English as a Second Language. Some seek that "cookbook" full of those extra special, unique lesson plans that will do the trick. This becomes even more valuable when the classroom includes a diverse group of students - some "normal learners," some challenged by learning differences (high or low achievers), students with language issues, and some who have physical, developmental, or sensory deficits.

One of the most common special accommodations stipulated in the Individual Education Plans of students who require them is the use of a computer and associated software, usually including word processing capabilities. Unfortunately, many IEP's do not stipulate how the word processors will be employed so that they actually facilitate learning and make it an easier process for the student. There are some IEP's which promote use of a computer in ways that will never happen in the day-to-day life of the student in school, because the intended procedures will take up too much time. Therefore, it makes tremendous sense to design an instructional model that makes use of this technology in ways that will actually help!

In developing this model, we worked from the basic assumption that a student will not feel confident in writing at higher levels until the ability to write a well-developed sentence has been mastered. Moreover, we wanted to insure that we gave students the language of instruction—an understanding of key terms that they would use to learn the steps of the model as well as receive feedback about their work within the model. As every teacher knows, the suggestion to "make it better" does not yield much in terms of improved student writing. "Fix it." Fix what? Every student we have asked remembers this type of scenario happening…

What follows is simple.

Unfortunately, this is a reason why some experienced English teachers, after hearing a cursory explanation, balk at using it. The process seems too simple.

However, we have worked with other teachers who have taken the time to understand fully the model and the reasons for its use, and they have made Word Forging® one of the first lessons of every new school year. This is the reason why your author trusts you will read this entire text before implementing the model. This method goes contrary to some tenets of instruction with which many of you have grown up. Give it a chance, and see if it works for you and your students.

When a blacksmith forges a piece of iron into a desired shape, it is a process. He or she heats the metal, pounds it toward a general shaping, heats it some more, pounds it again to shape it more specifically, heats it again, and continues the process until the final shape is achieved. It is not always a good idea to go too fast. The blacksmith desires the piece of wrought iron to stand the test of time.

Effective writing, in our opinion, entails a very similar process. A student writer can start by just writing down or typing basic ideas into simple sentences. The focus at this point is creativity or the brainstorming of ideas associated with the topic. Then, some of these ideas and shaped into sentences; in some cases, sentences can be combined. More details and information can be added so that the sentences become increasingly interesting and informative. Choice of vocabulary can be made at a more mature level. Lastly, adjectives and adverbs can be added so that the piece becomes more colorful and descriptive. At each step of the process, the writer can check the grade level to insure that such changes do in fact result in improvements.

Therefore, a simple three-step process is derived. Below is a pictorial representation that helps students as well as teachers to remember its elements:

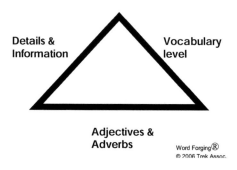

Word Forging®
© 2006 Trek Assoc.

(Oh, look – another triangle!!! Do you remember why? If not, recheck the chapter on the Triad Intervention[SM].)

The student writes some ideas in basic sentences to express his or her ideas. This is a brainstorming, right-brained activity (more on this topic later). Then the Word Forging® process is followed. First, the writer adds some details and information to improve the content. Second, the author reviews the language in his or her sentences so that more expressive synonyms and a higher, more mature level of vocabulary are employed. Finally, the sentences are revised so that colorful adjectives and adverbs can be added to the sentence in ways that add to their impact in meaningful and useful ways. Much of these later steps are left-brained activities. The entire process utilizes all parts of the brain, to optimize our potential to use our maximum intellect. (We will return later to a further discussion of the left-right brain issues.)

There is another element of Word Forging®, a very important use of the basic technology that is present but untapped in most classrooms in America today. When your author demonstrated this process one day to the Assistant Superintendent of a suburban school district, the administrator immediately noted the benefit of not having to run out and purchase completely new software for his schools. It was already there, but clearly underutilized. In fact, most teachers and certainly most students are likely not aware of the following information.

There is a hidden treasure in computers all over this country, and few people know about it!

Many word processors today have a number of features, some useful on an everyday basis and some rather obscure. Most word processor users are not aware of all of them. We usually know that we can perform manipulations of font, character spacing, centering, the number of columns, and margins. We happily go about the tasks of cutting/pasting, finding/replacing, inserting words and pictures, and using frames and special  presentation features that will make our work stand out from the usual and mundane. We can also do those valuable insertion and deletion tasks that save us so much time when compared to our pre-1980 writing efforts. (I still groan when I remember my typing-for-beer money efforts in college...) That computer salesman who sold your author his first personal computer in 1984 may have, in fact, been correct when he said that the computer would save us a lot of time (at least when it came to writing), but I doubt he knew why.

There are a number of methods to determine the reading level (such as grade level) of a book or composition. Each of these approaches looks at aspects which are considered important by their developers, and there may be some variation in scores from system to system. Edward Fry, of the Rutgers University Reading Center, created a widely used readability graph for use by educators (Fry, 1968). The calculations are based on the average number of syllables and the average number of sentences in a 100-word selection of a text. The Gunning FOG Index (Gunning, 1952) looks at samples of 100 words, counting the number of words, sentences, "big words" (three or more syllables), the average sentence length, the average percentage of "big words," and applying some calculations to these figures. The Flesch Formula for Reading Ease (Flesch, 1948) and the Flesch-Kincaid Grade Level formula work well with upper elementary and secondary texts, examining the number of words, sentences, and syllables which are manipulated in formulas to derive a "reading ease" score (from elementary grades up to post graduate college level) and a grade level score up to 12.0. The exact procedures for calculating these scores can be found in many sources on the Internet. Although very long sections of a book could be analyzed, the best results are to examine approximately 100 word sections or separate paragraphs by scoring them and then deriving an average. A "readability" score of the text is generated. Caution must be emphasized – the Flesch-Kincaid grade level formula was never intended to be used as a diagnostic device; it was developed to determine if a piece of writing was appropriate calibrated for its intended audience. However, this score can also be useful when examining your own writing.

Unfortunately, it can be rather time consuming and tedious to generate text sample readability levels for all of our students. There is another way to generate these values.

Many word processors today have within their software the ability to calculate the readability level (grade level) of the composition on the screen. Both Microsoft® Word and Corel® WordPerfect® use the Flesch-Kincaid formula, and Microsoft® Word also provides calculations for the Flesch Reading Ease score. You can find out if your sentence, paragraph, essay, or thesis is written at the fourth, ninth, or twelfth grade level.

The Flesch Reading Ease Scale is widely used outside of educational settings. It calculates reading from 100 (easy) to zero (very difficult, college level and up). A score of 65 is considered the "Plain English Score."

Some may feel that this is not important information. Teachers who wish to motivate students will realize the potential value of this calculation ability. Teachers who wish to give students immediate feedback about their editing efforts will recognize the benefits of this measure. Teachers who want to promote their students' independence in the writing process will welcome the roadmap that has just been laid at their feet!

It is useful at times to tell a student the grade level of their writing sample when it is done. Just saying "It is 5.4 grade level" or "It is 8.9 grade level" is not enough. It is amazing, however, to observe students learn to use the grade-level calculation as a means of learning improved writing and editing skills in ways that make sense to them. By simply changing some settings of most of the most popular word processors, the user can unleash this powerful learning tool. (See Appendix A for information on how to set up a word processor such as Microsoft® Word or Corel® WordPerfect® to calculate grade levels using the Flesch Reading Ease Score and the Flesch-Kincaid Grade Level.)

Here, again, are the basic steps of the Word Forging® model:

1) Details – add information to the sentence
2) Vocabulary – employ a more mature, advanced vocabulary
3) Description – use more adjectives and adverbs

At each step, the writer checks the readability grade level and determines if more revision is needed.

For example, consider the following sentence:

"On Tuesday, the man drove his car home after he was done with work."

It is a nice sentence. It is a sentence that any high school student might include in a short story, but it is written at the third grade third month level (3.3). Not exactly high school material…

Now, let us add some detail to this sentence:

"On Tuesday, the teacher drove his car home after he was done with work at school."

This is written at the 4.6 grade level. Just by detailing who the man is (a teacher) and where he worked (at a school), we added 1.3 in grade level. Now, some further changes:

"On Tuesday, the teacher drove his automobile home after he finished work at school."

We performed the second step in our Word Forging® process – using a more mature vocabulary. We used "automobile" instead of "car," and we used "finished" instead of "was done with." Because of these two changes, our sentence is now at 7.5 grade level (+2.9 years). Simple. Students can use their own vocabulary skills or can learn to employ the word processor's synonym and thesaurus features to select higher-level vocabulary. The basic rule of thumb is that words with more letters or syllables usually are considered to be at a higher grade-level than shorter words.

The use of this step, "playing" with vocabulary selection until the best word is chosen, is actually great practice for a fundamental skill in school – using context to select words. If a choice was available either to teach a list of 20 vocabulary words per week or to teach the skill to use context clues to determine the meaning of novel and unfamiliar words, we would select the second option every time. For teachers who want to encourage their students to become true learners rather than just parrots, the question is a "no-brainer."

In our third step, we add some adjectives and adverbs. Pretend that we want to visualize this man going home, and more color to our description will make it easier to see this in our mind.

"On Tuesday, the tired teacher slowly drove his automobile home after he finished work at the elementary school."

Eleventh grade, and a nice sentence to boot...

Does this author want to finish the job and make the sentence to be twelfth grade? Sure – why not? The process is easy, after all. The sentence needs to be "forged" (worked and revised) a bit more, just like that hot piece of iron that the blacksmith works. Therefore, the author can go back and add some detail (where is this school?) and describe the car ("old" – no, let's say "ancient"), and then recheck the grade level:

"On Tuesday, the tired teacher slowly drove his ancient automobile home after he finished work at the Springfield elementary school."

This is a well-crafted, twelfth grade sentence.

At the paragraph level, the benefits of such an approach to writing become even more evident. Examine this first paragraph:

Buddy was happy about his master's decision to take him for a walk. It is funny how a dog can sense when its owner intends to reach for the leash and go to the door. Buddy really enjoyed that simple bit of routine. It was the highlight of his day.

This is a nice little paragraph, and at first glance, it is well written. If a high school student composed it, however, the teacher may wish to help the student develop a more mature paragraph. According to the Flesch-Kincaid grade level analysis, it is written at the 5.5 level. Here is the same short paragraph written at a 12.0 grade level, after it is improved with more detail, a higher level of vocabulary, some descriptive improvements, and slight reorganization of its sentences (combining two short sentences).

Buddy, a wiry and energetic dachshund, was always thrilled about his master's decision to exercise him on a daily walk. Sensing when his owner Matthew, a retired businessman, would reach for the leather leash and amble toward the door, Buddy enthusiastically jumped and circled his owner's feet. That little brown and black canine reveled in the simple routine, the highlight of his everyday existence.

Yes, we are aware that readability score may in fact not be the same as the writing level of a passage. Just because a child can read at the 5th grade level does not mean that child can be expected to write at that level. However, for the purposes of this model, we do not feel the need to split the hairs. Using the readability level of a passage is consistent with a desire to write a composition so that a reader would have to have skills at the target level in order to have success with the paragraph. That understanding is fine with us. In fact, Donald Graves and his associates discovered that very young children could write <u>before</u> they can read because they usually learn to write anything they say (Graves, 1983). Teaching students to write sentences they have never said it a real challenge; teaching students to record on paper what they have said is much easier (some might even say it is fun).

When we are introducing the Word Forging® process to a new group of students, we explain the process and set the bar high. Instead of giving the students an overly challenging task to complete, we give them a challenge that motivates them! Ask them to take a sentence that does not even register at the first grade level and transform it into a twelfth grade sentence. Then, place a one-dollar bill on the table. The first student to reach the twelfth grade level with his or her sentence wins the dollar. What is the starting sentence? Something simple like "He saw it" or "She liked it."

In some of our schools, we also hold an Annual Writing Competition. We give all of the student participants the same short sentence (similar to the two above – a basic three-worder), and then we challenge them to write a sentence at the twelfth grade level using the Word Forging® procedures. If each student succeeds, then his or her sentence is added to the list of other successful entries. Finally, all sentences are collated into a list, names of authors are removed, and a pool of volunteer teachers vote for their favorite sentence – using whatever criteria they wish. (Some will focus on grammar, some on content, some on imaginative ideas, some on novelty, and some on their own unique values...) The student with the most votes wins. You would be amazed at the interesting sentences which are derived by the students. Your author is also gratified about the extent to which both the student authors and the staff judges enjoy the competition.

Here is another unique feature of this motivational technique. It does not usually matter at what grade level the authors are in school. Set the bar high. If you are working with elementary students, have them shoot for sixth or seventh grade. For our high school students, we ALWAYS set the bar at twelfth grade in practice sessions. This is true if the students are in advanced classes or in classes for students who learn differently than the norm.

In fact, students with learning differences (perhaps you know them as "learning [dis]abled students) appreciate this model of instruction. They have a concrete goal, they can try different things and get immediate feedback, and they have a plan that they understand. How do they fare in the writing instruction process that you usually use?

We must make a comment here about grade level determinations for the work of younger students. As Sharon Bradley-Johnson and Judi Lucas Lesiak state in <u>Problems in Written Expression: Assessment and Remediation</u>, it does not make much sense to assess for special education eligibility according to grade level of written expression below the third grade. In grades one and two, students focus primarily on handwriting, spelling, basic capitalization, and the more elementary punctuations rules. Many difficulties which might be detected most appropriately would be handled in the regular classroom through increased instruction. "Hence, even though it is possible to obtain a norm-referenced score to indicate a discrepancy in written expression prior to grade 3, judgment is needed to decide whether enough skills have been covered in the classroom to warrant special education" (Bradley-Johnson and Lesiak, 1989, p. 11). We would still maintain, however, that the procedures of Word Forging® can be used with students in grades below the third grade, but admittedly the Flesch-Kincaid grade level calculations below the 1.0 grade level seem to have limited utility in this approach. At third grade and above, students are asked to write with increased variety, skill, and purposes, so it makes sense to start any formal interventions with grade levels at that point.

Another issue must be remembered... A writer does not have to write at the twelfth grade level (or above) to be a good author. In fact, an effective writer often combines long and short sentences in order to have more variety in the content. Furthermore, sometimes the most expressive sentence in a novel can be just one word. Really! Many written communications are not appreciated because they are much too wordy and obtuse. Readers may just scan these messages or - worse – may not read them at all.

George Ehrenhaft, in his book entitled <u>Writing a Successful College Application Essay</u>, states, "Placing a tight, terse sentence next to a lengthy one creates a startling effect. The technique, however, works best when used rarely. Overuse dilutes its effect. Also, several short sentences in a row can be a tiresome as a string of long, complex sentences. A balance works best." (Ehrenhaft, 1993, p. 108)

It is important for an effective writer to know how to improve the level of one's writing when s/he desires to do so. An example of this is an eleventh or twelfth grader engaged in the process of applying to colleges. Does the student really want to submit an essay that is written at the sixth grade level?

We think not.

Try this process yourself. Take out that sentence about your day or your job – hopefully you wrote it as you were reading the start of this chapter – and type it into your computer's word processor on a blank page. Then, configure your software so it can calculate the grade level of your writing sample. (See Appendix A for the procedure to do this.) Look at the analysis. Surprised? Was it at the twelfth grade level or at whatever level you anticipated? If not, apply the Word Forging® methodology as you revise your work. Discover how you can add some details and information. Check the grade level again. Select a few words and make some alternative word choices so that you use more mature vocabulary. Re-calculate that grade level. Add a few color adjectives and adverbs that improve your imagery. Are you at twelfth grade yet? Then, re-examine the sentence (just like a blacksmith) and see if you can reshape it into an increasingly well-crafted piece of art.

Did you feel some innate motivation taking over? Did you enjoy finding out if the changes you made were beneficial or not? Could you anticipate yourself, with practice, making these steps more automatic? Can you appreciate how much more difficult this process of self-editing and improving your writing would have been in the pre-1980 world? Did you have at least a little fun going through this process?

When was the last time you were intrigued, motivated, and entertained by the process of improving your written expression?

To reiterate, here are the basic steps of this process:

1) **Add Details** – Increase the number of details in your sentence by adding information. You can do this by answering questions such as who, what, when, where, why, how, etc. You can also do it by combining two short but related sentences into a longer, cohesive sentence (thus increasing the number of words per sentence).

2) **Add Vocabulary** – Select a more mature vocabulary whenever possible. This is accomplished by using a thesaurus or the synonym feature of the word processor or (for younger students) by choosing words that have more syllables or letters.

3) **Add Color** – Insert meaningful and descriptive adjectives and adverbs which add to the content and linguistic density of the sentence without adding unnecessary wordiness.

The student writes down ideas into short and simple sentences, just to record them. Then, s/he goes through the three steps of Word Forging®. The student then checks the grade level of his or her composition at each step. If it is satisfactory, the work is done. If a higher grade-level is desired, the student has a choice of again doing step one, step two, or step three, or a combination of all three before checking the grade level again. The process is repeated (as a blacksmith works a piece of iron) until the final form of the sentence or passage is achieved.

The beauty of the approach is that the student can gauge the effectiveness of his or her own attempts immediately. The steps become more automatic after repeated practice. In fact, Word Forging® satisfies ALL of the requirements that your author set out when first considering the development of some approach that would help his students.

Here are some examples of sentences where the elements we are seeking have been neglected.

When a writer does not include enough detail, his or her sentence may look like this:

The man walked slowly over to the busy corner store to get some food and other things.

It is a reasonable sentence, but it lacks any detail; we have difficulty "picturing it in our minds." Based primarily on the number of words it contains, the sentence has a readability score of 6.3 grade level. Now, consider this revised sentence:

The widower walked slowly across the crosswalk on Smith Street in Springfield to the busy corner store to get some frozen dinners and fruit for his lonely dinner tonight.

This sentence, with a readability score of 12.0, has some nice details that help us imagine what is happening.

Here is another sentence, a variation (targeting vocabulary) of the original model we used:

The gentleman meandered slowly over to the busy corner supermarket to purchase some food and other necessities.

This sentence also has a readability score of 12.0.

Now is another variation (focusing on adding adjectives and adverbs) of the original sentence we used:

The gray-haired man walked slowly and painstakingly over to the busy corner store to get some dinner food and other necessary items.

This last sentence also has a readability score of 12.0.

Therefore, using any <u>one</u> of the elements of the Word Forging® model can result in a significant improvement in the readability score of the passage. When we combine aspects of all three elements (increased detail, higher vocabulary level, and increased use of descriptive adjectives and adverbs), we are able to produce the following improvement.

From this: *The man walked slowly over to the busy corner store to get some food and other things. (6.3)*

To this: *The gray-haired widower meandered painstakingly across the crosswalk on Smith Street in Springfield to the busy corner supermarket to purchase a frozen dinner, fruit, and other necessities for his lonely dinner tonight. (12.0)*

Some of the easiest ways to facilitate a student's use of more detail in his or her sentences is to ask the "W" questions – who, what, when, where, and why – as well as perhaps how. If the student writes about a girl, who is the girl? What is she doing? Where is she? Why is she doing what she is doing? How is she doing it? (This last question, how, may also lead to use of more adverbs, part of the last step in the Word Forging® model.)

It is a good idea to tell the writer to pretend that his or her reader knows <u>nothing</u> about the topic. When instructing students on a given writing assignment, your author would outlaw the words "thing" and "stuff" (as in "I went to the store to buy some things food for lunch and other stuff"). Their use adds very little to the idea density of the composition.

Another way to address the first step of the Word Forging® model (adding detail to the sentence = increasing the word count) is to combine two shorter sentences. This can be done simply by joining two independent clauses (sentences) by adding a comma after the first and a conjunction before the second, or by condensing the clauses:

The man had a hat. It was blue.
The man had a hat, and it was blue.
The man had a blue hat.

Conjunctions include words such as "and, but, so, or, yet, for, so" and others. One can also use adverb converters such as "because, although, when, until" and others. You can connect two shorter sentences with adverbial conjunctions such as "however" and "furthermore." If you desire to leave out these conjunctive words, you can also use a semi-colon:

The man had a hat; it was blue.

[Please note that when calculating the grade level of a sentence with two clauses separated by a colon, the word processor may consider this "two" sentences, resulting in lower grade level. Inserting a colon into a sentence, for example, may cause the computer to see "12:00" as significantly different that "twelve o'clock." The same is true when a space is not left between sentences. A higher grade level will be calculated.]

When we attempt to write more concisely, we can use certain transitional words to "mark" a conceptual change or movement in our sentences. Students should learn the types of transition words and how to use each in their writing:

o   Number/order – first, second, in the first place, next
o   Time – afterward, then, while, eventually, finally, at first, next
o   Degree of certainty – undoubtedly, perhaps, certainly, possibly
o   Location – here, next to, nearby, there, opposite, farther
o   Supporting a concept – furthermore, likewise, similarly, for example, again, on the contrary
o   Paragraph organization – first, then, next, finally, in the beginning, in the end, following that, the next step, throughout

There are many sources for information which expands on the above ideas (Kilborn, 2000; Ryan, 1996).

Many students (and some teachers) hate the study of grammar. They cringe whenever they are asked to recognize subordinate and main clauses. They get confused when one talks about active and passive voice. For some students, providing the rules of grammar can provide a structure and organization that benefits them. For others, they can learn how to combine sentences by performing the task repetitively, by getting more practice in doing it while explicitly being taught all of the applicable rules. One must also remember that in the Word Forging® model, we always keep in the back of our mind that every sentence does not need to be 25 words long. If we need the sentence to be complex or compound-complex in structure, we should know how to create it. If we want to vary the emphasis, pace, and impact of our sentences in an assignment, we should know how to do that also by including shorter sentences that fit the style we are attempting to create.

In the study of linguistics, the term "code switching" is used to denote the ability of a person to alter his or her use of language based on the demands of the listener or the situation. One clearly may want to employ a different type of language expression in meeting with a college professor than one might use on a sport playing field with best friends. Style, structure, and level of vocabulary may all be changed, based on communicative intent and need. The same should be true in written expression. The writer must be able to write with differing levels of formality based on the context of the writing act.

A word or two about the last step of the process – adding descriptive adjectives and adverbs. Rather than telling the reader what something is like, use words to have him or her taste, smell, hear, see, or feel the experience. Through repeated use of description, aspects of the character, place, or object are slowly revealed as if you were able to catch a longer and longer glimpse over time. Do not divulge all the description in the first sentence. Expose new information slowly, and use the senses to help the reader really experience what you are describing!

Do not belittle the fact that this Word Forging® process has only three steps. In fact, it was designed to be simple. Here is why... Think back to what you learned in school. You may remember who wrote <u>A Midsummer Night's Dream</u> (Shakespeare), where the Cradle of Civilization was (Mesopotamia), where in Chemistry class you would find a chart listing the elements (the periodic table), and what the first ten amendments to the Constitution of the United States are called (the Bill of Rights). However, what did your eighth grade English teacher tell you to do in order to improve your writing skills?

If you can now repeat our three steps to improve the writing of a sentence to a desired grade level, you have experienced your first success in the world of Word Forging®.

Congratulations!

V. WHY FOCUS FIRST ON THE SENTENCE?

As a Speech and Language Pathologist, your authors feels there might be others better qualified to work with students on effective paragraph development, the five-paragraph essay, and the finer points of writing an essay. It might be beneficial, however, for a student to work with the SLP to improve his or her use of the most basic element of the paragraph, the sentence.

We feel that before the advance levels of writing (types of essays, 5 paragraph essays, etc.) can effectively be addressed, it is valuable for the student to have the skill to write a well-crafted sentence. Upon that foundation, great compositions can be built. Obviously, one should not teach major essay writing skills until the student can write sentences first. The student will never progress in the development of longer and more complex writing samples unless he or she feels confident in that foundation skill.

If, for any reason, you do not believe this is true, test the hypothesis by looking at the work of a competent narrative author. Examine the sentences he or she uses. Then, look at the work of a person who struggles with written expression. You will likely note that your analysis comes back to the construction of faulty or acceptable sentences. Also, what is acceptable in sentence formulation in fourth grade may not be accepted in ninth grade. The skill of writing grade appropriate sentences needs to be taught, practiced, and perfected well beyond elementary school.

It is our opinion that unfortunately some instructional programs get a few samples of sentence writing and then move on to the next level without full automatization of the skills involved.

Steven Brust is a systems programmer for a computer manufacturer and a drummer for a suburban white reggae band. He is also an author. According to Eric Jorgensen, Brust was at a Seattle bookstore one evening and was overheard making a most profound statement about the art of written language. "The art of writing," Brust said, "is being able to write a good sentence." He contended that this was true for all forms of writing – novels, short stories, technical writing, and poetry. "If you can't write a good sentence," Brust said, "please do not show me your poetry"

(Jorgensen, 2000).

We can appreciate a well-crafted sentence, but it is sometimes difficult to decide why we like that sentence. Sometimes, or perhaps more often, it is easy to identify a sentence we do not like, but it is difficult to say *why* we dislike it. We like to learn some bit of information or get a feeling from the sentence, but we also want clarity. In "Attending to Style," Karen Gocsik states, "your reader does not want to wrestle with your sentences... Above all, she wants to feel that you, the writer, are doing the bulk of the work, and not she, the reader" (Gocsik, 2004). This article is a great source for the basic principles of the sentence and how to write a forceful and clear sentence. These basics include focusing on actors and actions, being concrete (except for abstract nouns but know when to use them), being concise, being coherent, being emphatic, being in control, and writing beautifully (Goczik, 2004). Please refer to this article for examples and expansion on these ideas, but we will re-examine these issues later when we construct our rubrics for analysis of writing samples.

Once construction of the sentence is mastered at a basic level, the student can then progress to the paragraph. When appropriate paragraphs can be formulated, the instruction can turn to the multi-paragraph essay. However, each of these elements must been seen within the context of the developmental or grade-appropriate skills. A sixth grader can create a wonderfully imaginative and complete five-paragraph essay about a trip to a zoo, but this may not be accepted as twelfth grade work by a high school senior. Each stage or level has its own measures and expectations.

Again, one of the sad realities is that many high school teachers feel that a student should have learned how to write effectively by middle school at the latest. This is one reason why some high school teachers have given up when it comes to teaching written expression – they feel that students should have mastered the topic a long, long time ago. (Or, maybe the teacher does not possess expert writing skills and does not feel qualified to teach others how to do it…)

Ruth Berry recently published some research that underscored the need of teachers to be aware of their personally held beliefs on their instructional decisions about writing and on their student's school experiences. The implementation of some well-defined instructional strategies and models (such as process writing) may be interpreted, implemented, and perhaps even impaired by the views of the teacher. There is potential, however, for a teacher's stylistic preferences to be preserved when some approaches are used (Berry 2006).

Years ago, research done by Hall (1981) suggested that poor writers usually relied on simple sentences. Thomas, Englert, and Gregg (1987) reported that 84% of the syntactical errors in the writing of sixth and seventh grade learning disabled students were due to the use of a phrase instead of a full sentence. We have known for quite a long time that writing an effective sentence is difficult for students who have language or learning disabilities.

A common complaint that we have heard in schools is that students cannot differentiate between a full sentence or a fragment. Even worse, we have been told that some students will never learn to do so – it seems "beyond" them. Recent research, however, shows that knowledge of the simplest grammar rules, which we used to think separated man from beast, can be taught to a bird (Fox News Network, 2006).

Once the student has mastered the basics of composing a well-written sentence, s/he can move on to the steps required in the creation of more advanced works. Basically, there are five steps in the process of a writing task:

1) Prewriting (organizing your thoughts)
2) Writing (putting thoughts in sentences and/or paragraphs)
3) Revising (reorganizing)
4) Editing (checking the grammar and language used)
5) Publishing (finalizing the work so it can be shown to other people in some fashion)

When one edits his or her own work, the goal is to find errors in the following areas and to correct them: spelling, capitalization, punctuation, use of grammar, sentence structure, and word usage. One should also check subject/verb agreement and consistent verb usage.

There are approaches, methods, programs, and texts which fine tune the steps above and also which expand on a student's ability to produce narratives, express opinions, compare and contrast, expose information, and debate topics in paragraphs, five paragraph essays, or major research papers. These are beyond the scope of our present topic, but suffice it to say (again) that all of these works have as their foundation the ability to compose a well-written sentence.

The Online Writing Lab (OWL) at Purdue University is an absolutely wonderful source for materials and approaches to be used in the instruction of written language. It should become a "best friend" of the writing instructor. We recommend that you visit their website to discover this resource, especially for higher level tasks.

As stated previously (but we need to repeat often), there is one caveat that we always make clear to our students. Just because you CAN write a sentence at the twelfth grade level does not mean all of your sentences need to be at that level. A good author varies sentence length to keep the reader's attention. Based on our audience's need, sometimes a short "sentence" is advantageous. Sometimes it is best, in fact. Required. (Do you get the point?) Knowing how to write a grade-appropriate sentence when you need to is the mark of a mature writer.

We need to continually remind ourselves and our students that revision is a great thing. Mastering the art of revision is quite an accomplishment. As James Michener once said, "I may be the world's worst writer, but I'm the world's best rewriter" (Andersen, 1994, p. 3).

VI. WORDINESS

It sounds great to say that all one has to do to improve the level of one's writing is to add words – details, vocabulary, and colorful adjectives and adverbs.

However, the art of writing (and the art of teaching others to write well) needs to include the avoidance of excessive wordiness. There are a number of books, articles, websites, and instructional manuals devoted to this topic. Here, we will attempt to highlight the most important points and strategies which we have found useful in our own work with students of various ages and abilities.

There are many people who fall within one of two camps – those who feel it is better to say in 100 words what you could otherwise say in only fifteen, and those who feel it is better to use fifteen words to say what you might want to explain in 100. Our goal is to help our students develop the strategies to find the happy medium. An effective writer avoids unnecessary words. Using too many words to express yourself results in your reader being bored or confused.

It is important to remember that there are some steps in the writing process which are meant to be free, uncontrolled, and imperfect. Accepting that fact can liberate the writer to try some new things. The skills of revising and editing, however, are the "lost skills" of writing for many of today's high school students. They do not know how to edit, and they hate revising. Like most other skills, the more you write – and edit and revise and write again – the better you will become at it.

We do not want our written expression to contain too many or unneeded words. There are steps that can be taught which minimize excessive wordiness. We often say in five words that which we could say in one or two well-chosen words. Kathy McGinty provides a tongue in cheek approach to bulking up our sentences with unnecessary written verbiage (McGinty, undated). Some examples of her recommended steps include referring to studies even if you are not aware of any studies, replacing simple words with multisyllable words of Latin or Greek origin, using vague phrases, using classic redundancies, inserting "it is" or "there are" unnecessarily, and using adjectives which lengthen the sentence but which add no meaning to it.

Jennifer Jordan-Henley has prepared an interesting list of "clutter words" that frequently appear in business and technical writing. For example, we do not really need to write about "absolute guarantees, advance reservations, any and all, 12 noon or 12 midnight, close proximities, estimations of about, filled capacities, or first priorities." Some of these sayings are quite amusing if one really thinks about them, so I recommend you find this list and read it (Jordan-Henley, undated). The Online Writing Lab at Purdue University also cites the problems with redundant pairs: basic fundamentals, true facts, important essentials, final outcome, past history, etc. (OWLS, 2004).

We might add some other rules of thumb when it comes to reducing clutter and redundancy in written expression. Some of these are included in Jack Rawlin's The Writer's Way (Rawlins, 1992) and the Online Writing Lab at Purdue University (OWLS, 2004). Consider these recommendations:

1) Avoid the use of "I …" constructions in paragraphs or essays of opinion (ex. – I feel that it is extremely important to write clearly). Just state the opinion (ex. – Clear writing is extremely important). In many instances, the word "that" is a red flag to wordiness…

2) Watch use of the verb "to be." Use simple action verbs instead of "is" verb forms (ex. – "travels" instead of "is traveling"). Avoid starting sentences with "there is," "there are," etc. Avoid adjectives which follow "who is" or "who are" ("The man who is elderly…" can be restated as "the elderly man…"). Avoid using "to be" when possible ("He was thought to be an excellent football player" can be restated as "He was an excellent football player"). Use

active rather than passive verbs ("the food was purchased by the woman" can become "the woman purchased the food"). Avoid expletive or filler words such as "it is," "there is," "which is," "that is," and similar words when possible. (Example: "We have had a good meal today, and it is clear that people left the table satisfied." versus "Everyone had a good meal today and left the table clearly satisfied.")

3) If you have two sentences that are closely related, try to isolate "what's new" in the second sentence. Then add that new fact to the first sentence and cut the rest.

4) Avoid compound words or phrases in pairs in redundant ways (ex. – essential and important, innovative and new, vicious and brutal, like and enjoy, etc.)

5) Avoid repeating words unless you absolutely, absolutely, absolutely need to do so. (Enough said…)

6) Avoid slang, colloquial ("ain't"), regional, technical, and overly scholarly language as their use may confuse some readers. (Some students dislike reading some Mark Twain books because of the language, but they sometimes find the task easier when the book is read aloud. It may be easier to hear the words of Huckleberry Finn rather than read them.)

7) Avoid unnecessary description words if they do not add to the image. Change phrases into single words when possible ("the man with the most athletic abilities…" can be restated as "the most athletic man").

One caveat – do not become boring. Be careful about trimming everything. As Rawlins states, "Efficiency in writing is like efficiency in the workplace: It's a good thing, but it's not everything. When efficiency makes us robotic, life isn't worth living" (Rawlins, 1992, 206). There is a place for color in our lives.

A good rule of thumb to use is to "make every word count."

Some other useful hints include the following:

✓ Use vocabulary at your comfort level. If you are

not sure of a word's meaning, do not use it. *Beware of the computer word processor's spell check and grammar check functions, as they are not fool proof.* Also, be careful when selecting a word from a number of options. Too often, students select a word that "looks" good but is not, and the sense of the sentence is disrupted.

✓ Avoid passive verb constructions ("Little league teams are being coached by fathers all over this country." versus "Fathers coach little league teams all over the country.") Some word processors can be configured to tell the writer the percentage of passive sentences that are included in their composition. If it is too high, then the work may be more confusing and convoluted than it needs to be.

✓ Avoid references to yourself in an essay. ("I believe…" or "It is my opinion that…") Every comment you make is your opinion.

✓ When possible, combine two or more shorter, related sentences into one longer but more concise one ("The boy swung the bat. He hit the ball. He ran to first base." versus "The boy swung his bat, hit the ball, and ran to first base.")

There should be an emphasis on fluency; just get the students to write – a lot! Get ideas down on paper. Then work to improve the grammar, spelling, and mechanics. Give the students a scaffold or plan to follow, helping intimidated students feel that they actually can do this! Process writing mirrors the approach that experienced writers use (Allen, 2003).

Regina Richards presents a number of useful articles about writing skills, compensatory approaches, teaching strategies, and other topics on the LDOnline.org websites. To exemplify how care must be taken when using a computer word processor's spell checker, Ms. Richards cites the following little poem about computer spell checkers which she obtained from the Internet (with author unknown):

Eye halve a spelling chequer
It came with my pea sea
It plainly marques four my revue
Miss steaks eye kin knot sea.

Eye strike a key and type a word
And weight four it two say
Weather eye am wrong oar write
It shows me strait a weigh.

As soon as a mist ache is maid
It nose bee fore two long
And eye can put the error rite
Its rare lea ever wrong.

Eye have run this poem threw it
I am shore your please two no
Its letter perfect awl the weigh
My chequer toll me sew.

(Richards, 1999)

We do not believe that any skill can be left completely to software, the computer, some fancy videotaped demonstrations, or a commercial program. There will always be a role for the human teacher to interject the art of teaching into the equation. Knowing how, when, and how much to get between a student and his/her writing is an art. We do know, however, that interfering too much will result in the student's assuming less and less responsibility for his/her own work.

The Word Forging® Game (described in this text) is a great activity to teach students that the foremost skill in writing more mature sentences is vocabulary selection. *Adding many words may or may not add to the grade level of one's work.*

VII. CORRECTING STUDENT WORK

Here is a common scenario. A student works on an essay or paper, and she turns her final copy into the teacher for grading. The teacher reviews the work, and he makes a number of marks in various places on the manuscript, denoting corrections that should be made for sentence sense, word usage, capitalization, punctuation, spelling, and/or organizational structure. He may just deduct "points" from the grade he will assign to the girl's paper, or perhaps he is feeling particularly benevolent today. This time, he will return the paper to the girl, advising that she make the corrections he has noted and allowing her to resubmit the essay for a better final grade.

What a nice teacher. He is helpful to the student, highlighting her errors and giving her a chance to fix them for a better grade. He is really promoting learning.

Wrong.

Remember the Dedication of this book. (You may wish to reread it at this time.) In ninth grade at Locust Valley High School on Long Island, New York, I had an English teacher by the name of Mrs. Roberta Bishop. When you were finishing the eighth grade and received your schedule for the coming year, you first looked at the English class section. If you had a name other than "Bishop," you breathed a sigh of relief. If you saw the word "Bishop" in the teacher column, you might lose control of some important bodily functions. Mrs. Bishop's reputation definitely preceded her.

We thought her to be a tyrant. She yelled, walked around the room with her small spiral pad upon which she made her notes, and when the bell rang, she would read off the names of the unfortunate ones who were required to come see her after school that day. The doomed had to continue through the day, worrying, and then go to Mrs. Bishop's classroom after school to be informed of the great transgression they had committed earlier in English class that day. It might have been talking while she had been talking. It might have been incomplete or shoddy homework. It might have been a completely wrong answer for a query about today's reading. It might have been a missing end quotation mark on sentence number seven of last night's homework. You never knew for sure until you reported for the after school session. Then, the charge would be read, and skipping right over the trial aspect of this procedure (as you were always guilty, of course), you would hear the punishment – write "I will end every question with a question mark" fifty times, or some such task. When you were done, you could leave. No great explanation or discussion; you just wanted out of there.

There was something worse, however. Each quarter, students in Mrs. Bishop's class had to submit their notebooks for her review. These were thick (growing thicker each quarter) loose-leaf notebooks filled with homework assignments, classroom notes, study guides and questions/responses, and our essay or poetry assignments. Each student would turn in the notebook and wait until the next day's class to get the verdict – it was graded either as an "A" or a zero. Nothing in between. No gray areas. It

was either acceptable or it was not. If Mrs. Bishop found even one small punctuation error in your class notes form October 17th's lecture about <u>The Midsummer Night's Dream</u>, you received a zero. The problem was she never marked the error. You just knew that there was something wrong <u>somewhere</u> in your notebook. Your job that evening was to find it.

Usually, the student did find an error (it could be a coin toss as to whether the error you found was the same one found by Mrs. Bishop earlier that day). Sometimes you found a few of them, and breathed a sigh of relief. You would bring your notebook into class the next day and she would start looking through it again. (Mrs. Bishop had this uncanny skill of remembering where most students had made their error in her previous review of the notebooks.) You watched, barely breathing, as she leafed through your notebook. Then she would calmly close it, turn to the first page, and write either a big "A" or a big zero on the page. If you scored a zero, the process of hunting for the error(s) began again.

It was torture.

However, students in Mrs. Bishop's classes learned grammar, capitalization, punctuation, and paragraph organization. I learned it so well, in fact, that students in college often asked me to look over their papers to see if I could catch any obvious errors. It was easy for me to make much of my spending money in college by typing other people's papers on my old IBM Selectric.

Years later, I was happy that I had Mrs. Bishop as my teacher because she had not done one thing for me. She had not "fixed" my papers and compositions for me. She forced me to learn the rules of English so that I could fix them myself. What a truly wonderful gift...

Many teachers merely mark errors in student writing samples by underlining, circling, or otherwise highlighting the error. Others just go ahead and make the corrections for the student to see. There are commonly used proofreader marks that can be taught to students so that teachers will devote less time to corrections. These include:

≡ (under a letter)	capitalize a lower case letter
/ (slash through a letter)	use lower case instead of capital letter
¶	start new paragraph
^	insert
ℓ	delete

However, before we go too far into a discussion of such symbols for editing, we need to consider why and how we are responding to the work our students produce.

Karen Gocsik, Executive Director of Dartmouth College's Writing Program, presents a wealth of useful information on the Dartmouth Writing Program website. I advise you visit that website. In her article, "Responding to Student Text" (Gocsik, 2005), she makes recommendations to college professors about operational steps in correcting student papers, including the hiring of a writing assistant to specifically review drafts of student papers. She gives ideas for examining the thesis, structure, coherence of the paragraphs, and style parameters. She includes a very worthwhile section on the types of responses professors can provide to their students once any problems have been identified in a writing assignment. These responses include:

- ➤ Facilitative
- ➤ Directive
- ➤ Corrective
- ➤ Evaluative

It is wise to try to incorporate all of these. Corrective comments or marks are very familiar to many teachers. They label or circle errors, or they actually rewrite the sentence to make it correct. However, when a professor simply corrects student mistakes, the students get into the habit of merely "fixing" the work so it meets the professor's expectations. Facilitative remarks are often questions ("What are you trying to say here?" or "Can you provide some details?"); the professor puts the responsibility of improvement back on the student. No explicit directions for revision are provided. Directive remarks tell a student what to do – "move this paragraph" "omit that sentence" – in order to improve the paper. Evaluative responses usually are the grade the student receives on the composition. When looking at an evaluative comment about the paper, the emphasis is usually on content rather than form. The professor can make feedback comments in the margins throughout the paper or reserve them for the last page of the essay/paper. It is important to remember to insert positive comments or praise throughout the paper (research shows professors often spend more time on the negative side rather than the positive side of their remarks). We consider these some great perspectives on the act of responding to student text, and once more we advise you do some research on the Dartmouth Writing Program's website.

To these excellent recommendations, we would add one more – a variation on Mrs. Bishop's approach of 1967. It has also been described in an excellent article entitled "Minimal Marking" (Haswell, 1983). This author maintained that no research has shown conclusively that corrective marking of student papers really has much effect on student writing in the long term. Haswell detailed an approach, which admittedly had been "around" for while (since then 1940's or before) which resulted in immediate improvements. He recommends that all errors in a student's text be left unmarked within the text itself. Instead, he proposed that all punctuation, capitalization, spelling, and grammar errors be indicated by a simple check mark made by the teacher in the margin of the paper, on the line in which the error occurs. Multiple check marks in a single line indicate multiple errors in that line. Until a student has made the corrections indicated, no grade is recorded. This approach requires much less of the teacher's time, and it allows the teacher quickly to mark "surface errors" while focusing more on content. Haswell reported that students generally find 60-70% of their errors without major intervention. When minimal marks are made on a page of text, students tend to be less overloaded with correction information. Such an approach presents a puzzle to the student (where is the error?) and reinforces the use of a search and find strategy. Finally, Haswell states the approach is self-motivating as students work to eliminate any teacher check marks on their papers and to get the grade for the paper. Students who have not eliminated the checks will not get a grade and need to keep editing... Progress is observed over a semester of intervention using this approach, especially if the teacher records the initial number of checks on each paper - "John, at the beginning of the year you had 10-12 checks on each paper, but now you average around 4-5... Great job!" Further, when a few consistent check marks persist in later papers, they usually suggest that the student does not understand some rule or principle of writing which hopefully can then be isolated and taught effectively. As Haswell notes, Comenius once stated, *"the more the teacher teaches, the less the student learns."* We need to give students back the responsibility for their progress in written expression as they mature.

Some parents or teachers may feel that the use of simple check marks may be too vague for their students (particularly younger ones) who are attempting to learn and implement rules of English. Therefore, we would suggest the following compromise.

Instead of making just check marks or those varied corrective remarks which we anticipate the student will see and correct in the final draft (thereby learning primarily just to correct what we say is wrong, and fix it the way we tell them), we recommend that the teacher mark in the margins the following symbols, especially for younger students:

P = punctuation error
C = capitalization error
S = spelling error
V = word choice/vocabulary error
SS = sentence sense error
St = paragraph structure error
Any facilitative comments you might add to get the student to think about what is needed to make the assignment better.

We highlight that an error exists. It is up to the student to find it and correct it. Try this approach with your students' written essays. It will reduce the time it takes for you do to make your assignment reviews, and it places the burden of correction back on your student. Here is a sample:

The man got up early and he went to his job at the schol.	P S
He arrived at the parking lot and revealed that someone	V
had taken his parking spot he was not happy. The man	SS P
worked at Palmer High School.	St -
	Story ending?

The student should take the essay and either detect the errors to which the referred or ask for assistance and explanation. It is hoped that he or she will be able to resubmit the following essay:

The man got up early, and he went to his job at Palmer High School. He arrived at the parking lot and discovered that someone had taken his parking spot. He was not happy. The man complained to the school principal when he entered the school office.

To save time, it is also wise to begin to accumulate worksheets that target a specific writing skill issue such as end punctuation, common homonyms and their use, use of quotation marks, combining sentences, etc. Instead of having to explain verbally to each student in a class who is unsure of the problem issue, a teacher could hand out a sheet that fully explains the item and provides practice exercises. One does not have to re-invent the wheel for each new student. An alternative approach would be to record common issues that student are having, and then the teacher could hold extra help sessions that target each particular problem.

Also, it might be wise to offer a grade to the student for his or her paper as presented. Then, the teacher may offer extra credit only if the student works to revise the paper's grammar, spelling, and punctuation errors as indicated by the margin check marks. With older students, we like Haswell's idea of the check marks because they put even more responsibility on the student.

One of the most challenging tasks in writing is to do an effective job of proofreading one's own work. It is often difficult to do this immediately after composing a paragraph or essay, as we tend to perceive what we <u>think we wrote</u> rather than what we actually did write.

Let us give you an example of why this is. One of the perceptual processes that humans employ in their daily lives is the skill of closure – auditory or visual. This process involves the "filling in" of blanks or gaps in what we hear or see, making sense of the parts or bits even when there is something missing. We are able to get meaning from what we might consider nonsense if we were paying more attention. Consider the following paragraph. Can you make sense of it?

A dog want down tha lana and found a bona. Ha likad bonas and wantad to sava this ona to anjoy it fully. Ha carriad in homa quickly, navar latting it laava his mouth. Ha placad in carafully in his doghousa. Ha movad his blankat around so that tha bona would ba hiddan from anyona or anything that lookad into tha doghousa. Tha dog than laft to axplora around tha naighborhood again. Whan ha cama homa finally, ha want to ratriava his bona. Savaral hours wara spant savoring tha tasta and aroma of that bona. Ovarall, it had baan a good day.

It sounds a bit Italian, doesn't it? Actually, all the "e" vowels were replaced by "a" vowels. Here is the corrected passage:

A dog went down the lane and found a bone. He liked bones and wanted to save this one to enjoy it fully. He carried in home quickly, never letting it leave his mouth. He placed in carefully in his doghouse. He moved his blanket around so that the bone would be hidden from anyone or anything that looked into the doghouse. The dog then left to explore around the neighborhood again. When he came home finally, he went to retrieve his bone. Several hours were spent savoring the taste and aroma of that bone. Overall, it had been a good day.

You probably were able to make sense out of the first paragraph after getting used to reading the pattern. Just as in this exercise, we often "get used to" our mistakes soon after writing them.

Another mental process is called scanning. We can visually scan a section of writing yet not find all that we are attempting to find. In this box, how many f's are there?

t	*f*	*r*	*o*	*j*	*f*	*e*	*x*	*r* *F* *N*

The man who was first in line went to the store to find the name of the owner.

elephant	*farmer*	*treehouse*	*Newfoundland*	*face*	*with*

r	*n*	*o*	*b*	*a*	*p*	*h*	*c*	*f*	*b*	*q* *t*

shoe   knowledge   coffeehouse   manpower   exploration   fun

There are thirteen "f" consonants in the box. Finding them all involves effective scanning. Visual scanning is involved in finding all the punctuation marks in an essay, or looking through a text to find all the dates, etc. We often miss the target items when we try right after completing a writing assignment.

It is often useful to put away the work and return to it a day later, re-reading it as if it were new and novel. We usually catch more of our errors that way. Another suggestion is to read the work aloud, as we tend to pay more attention to the printed word when we orally decode rather than when reading silently. Another good idea is to read the words backwards – it works for some people. Covering up the page with a piece of paper so that we can only see one line at a time is another task that works for some people. Interesting, covering the page with a colored plastic sheet can also help some people identify errors more readily. It is important that each writer find the proofreading methodology that works best for him or her.

A useful protocol for reviewing the text composed by students is by the process of peer editing. The teacher develops a list of standards or expectations which one student should use to review the work completed by another student. These standards can be formulated into a chart or rubric that clarifies what the student reviewers should be evaluating. The rubric can be very basic, as in the case of elementary students, or rather complex at the college level.

Having students review each other's work facilitates learning by 1) identifying errors when they occur, thus improving the skills of proofreading and editing, 2) facilitating discussion about writing among students, and 3) making expectations clearer.

Elements that might be included in a peer-editing worksheet for younger students would include:

- Name on paper
- Following directions, including all required parts
- Complete sentences
- Correct grammar (with target elements specified)
- Correct spelling
- Correct capitalization
- Indentation of new paragraphs
- Organization of paragraphs (topic sentence, body, conclusion, etc.)
- Proofreading

The rubric for younger students can be quite informal and

fun. Smiley faces can be employed (☺). Because the progression skills in the younger can be quite different over the course of a school year, the rubric employed at the end of the year may be much more in-depth and detailed than the one used at the start of the year. It is useful to keep in mind that all elements of the rubric should be in the realm of developmentally appropriate success for the students. It makes no sense to use a fourth-grade writing rubric for second-grade students unless you are intent on causing frustration and dislike for the act of writing. A good teacher encourages success and growth in competency. Good students become better students when they are clear about what they are supposed to be learning.

A rubric for older students might also include elements such as inclusion of necessary details to make your point, cohesiveness (no unnecessary details), logical organization, use of descriptive words, use of mature vocabulary, varied sentence types, neatness of presentation, length of paper (3 paragraphs, 5 pages, etc.), use of sources, citing of sources, and others.

There are four basic types of paragraphs or essays, based primarily on the purpose for writing:

Descriptive – describing, creating an image, or "painting a picture" of something
Narrative – telling a story or telling about an event
Expository – explaining how to, explaining causes, detailing types or kinds, and defining a term or concept
Persuasive – attempting to change another person's opinion or behavior

Each will have a slightly different type of rubric for evaluative purposes.

It is important that each rubric also include a section where the reviewer (peer or adult teacher) can include some personalized comments to highlight the evaluative function of the review. Remember – use of positive comments in an overview of the text is also a great idea. Catch them being good!

Some examples of rubrics for both teacher review and

peer editing are available in the <u>Word Forging® Companion</u>.

One last word about the teacher correction of students' written work. It is NOT solely the job of the English teacher. There is much current literature and research about the methods of "writing to learn" which are beyond the scope of this book, but which deserve the attention of all classroom teachers. When students write about topics you are hoping they will learn, they begin to take ownership of those ideas and lessons. It has been said that some teachers foster the demonstration of learning disabilities by focusing on what students cannot do, deficits rather than strengths. Process writing focuses on what students know, teaching skills in specific contexts. As students see the need, skills are taught (Stinger, 1999). Process writing is "a writing instruction model that views writing as an ongoing process… in which students follow a given set of procedures for planning, drafting, revising, editing, and publishing their writing" (Harris and Hodges, 1995, p. 195).

There are specific expectations and considerations that are relevant to college-level composition. <u>The Nuts and Bolts of College Writing</u> (Harvey, 2003) and <u>Nuts & Bolts: A practical guide to teaching college composition</u> (Newkirk, ed., 1993) are two good sources for students and teachers at that level. The focus at the college level is much more on content than on style, so further discussion is beyond the central scope of the current text. However, there are some important aspects to remember: 1) good writing at the college level continues to have as a foundation the ability to write effective sentences, and 2) the importance of revision, self-editing, and proofreading. As Harvey states, "an essay is written on paper, not carved in stone" (Harvey, 2003, p. ix). We want to encourage college students to feel that they have important things to write about. Susan Wheeler, in "Exercises for Discovery, Experiment, Skills, and Play" in <u>Nuts & Bolds: A practical guide to teaching college composition</u> (Newkirk, ed., 1993, p. 71), we want students to "experience the energy of writing honestly."

VIII. EXAMPLES OF PARAGRAPHS
AT GRADE LEVELS

3.0

Suzanne went to her friend's home to play. The girls played all day
with their many dolls. The friend's mother gave the girls some
cups of cold grape juice. Suzanne had a fun day, but then she had
to go back to her own home again.

4.0

One day, Suzanne went to her friend's home to play. The girls
played house all day with their many dolls. The friend's mother
gave the girls some cups of cold grape juice. Suzanne had a fun
day, but then she had to go back to her own home again because
she heard Mother calling.

5.0

One day, Suzanne went to her friend's home to play. The girls
played make-believe house all day with their many dolls. The
friend's mother gave the girls some cups of cold grape juice.
Suzanne had a fun day, but then she had to go back to her own
home again because she heard Mother calling for dinner.

6.0

One day, Suzanne went to her friend's home on Springfield Street
to play. The girls played make-believe house all day with all of
their dolls. In midafternoon, the friend's mother gave them cups
of delicious cold grape juice. Suzanne had a fun day, but then she
returned home because she heard Mother calling for dinner.

7.0

On a lazy Wednesday, Suzanne went to her best friend's home on Springfield Street to play. The girls played make-believe house with their favorite dolls. In the midafternoon, the friend's mother treated them to iced grape juice cups. Suzanne had a fun afternoon but left when Mother shouted, "Dinner!"

8.0

On a lazy Wednesday during summer vacation, Suzanne went to her best friend's home on Springfield Street to play. The girls played make-believe house with their favorite dolls. In the midafternoon, the friend's mother treated them to iced grape juice cups. Suzanne had a fun afternoon but left quickly when Mother shouted, "Dinner!"

9.0

On a lazy Wednesday during summer vacation, Suzanne went to her best friend's home on Springfield Street to play. The girls played make-believe house with their favorite dolls. In the midafternoon, the friend's mother treated them to iced grape juice cups. Suzanne had an enjoyable afternoon but departed quickly when she heard her Mother shouting, "Dinner!"

10.0

On a lazy Wednesday during summer vacation, Suzanne walked to her best friend's home on Springfield Street to play. Suzanne and Mary played make-believe house with their favorite dolls. In the midafternoon, the friend's mother treated the children to some iced grape juice cups. Suzanne had an enjoyable afternoon but departed hurriedly when she heard her Mother shouting loudly from the back door, "Dinner!"

11.0

On a lazy Wednesday during summer vacation, Suzanne walked quickly to her best friend's home on nearby Springfield Street to play. Suzanne and Mary played games of make-believe house with their favorite dolls. In the middle of the blistering hot afternoon, the friend's mother treated the children to some flavorful iced grape juice cups. Suzanne had a pleasurable afternoon but departed hurriedly when she heard her Mother shouting loudly from their back door, "Suzanne - Dinner!"

12.0

On a lazy Wednesday during summer vacation, Suzanne walked quickly to her best friend's home on nearby Springfield Street to play. Suzanne and Mary enjoyed games of make-believe house with their favorite dolls. In the middle of the blistering hot afternoon, Mary's mother treated the busy children to some flavorful iced grape juice cups. Suzanne had a pleasurable afternoon in a fantasy world with Mary and their mystical dolls, but she departed hurriedly when she heard her Mother shouting loudly from their back door, "Suzanne - Dinner!"

COLLEGE LEVEL

It was a lazy Wednesday during summer vacation when Suzanne walked quickly to the home of her best friend, Mary, on nearby Springfield Street to enjoy games of make-believe house with their favorite dolls. In the middle of the blistering hot afternoon, Mary's mother interrupted the busy children to treat them to some flavorful iced grape juice cups. Suzanne experienced a pleasurable, fantasy-filled afternoon with Mary and their dolls in fancy outfits, but as she anticipated her father's arrival at home this evening with a new purebred Labrador puppy for her family, she departed hurriedly when she heard her Mother shouting loudly from their back door, "Suzanne – Come home immediately!"

IX. THE DISORDER OF WRITTEN EXPRESSION

Sometimes, the problems that a person might experience in written expression go beyond the lack of practice or ineffective instructional practices. There are so many skills incorporated into written expression that is sometimes difficult to keep track of them all. Being able to write well is often considered a requirement for academic progress. Teachers frequently look at the status of a student's being an effective or ineffective writer as a hallmark of potential achievement in the classroom. Sadly, writing is a huge obstacle for some students due to the presence of a difference in learning or ineffective past instruction.

Unfortunately, it is often difficult to determine if a student's difficulties are due to a specific disability in written expression or in one of the other related skill areas – cognitive, language, and sensorimotor. Is it a problem of spelling, illegible handwriting, organization and sequencing, dyslexia, or language processing? There may be issues related to neurobiology, neuropsychology (including memory, attention, visual-spatial, etc.), genetics (family history, fetal alcohol syndrome), and other aspects. Because of these difficulties in isolating aspects of this issue, demographic data is also hard to accumulate. It has been said that 8 to 15% of the general population demonstrates some form of a learning disability in written expression (Lyon, 1996).

We know of some important historical figures who may have suffered from a deficit of written expression. Thomas Alva Edison was unable to read until he was twelve years old, and his writing skills continued to be poor throughout his life. George Washington was unable to spell well, and his grammar usage skills were very poor. His brother suggested that the best career for him might have been a backwoods surveyor.

The Diagnostic and Statistical Manual of Mental Disorders, 4th edition, characterizes a Disorder of Written Expression as one of the learning disorders. It specifies that the person must have writing skills substantially below those expected for his/her age, resulting from significant interference with academic achievement and/or the activities of daily living that require the composition of texts. It can coexist with sensory, motor, neurological, and intellectual conditions, but the effects of a writing disability must be in excess of the traits usually associated with the other conditions. (DSM-IV, 1994). A psychoeducational evaluation is usually required, and care must be taken to insure a true differential diagnosis (Luttinger and Gertner, 2005). It must be noted, however, that the DSM-IV states that there is no proven effective treatment for a disorder of written expression.

Disabilities which can be considered comorbid (co-existing) with written expression deficits can include the following:

- ✓ Dyslexia
- ✓ Dysgraphia
- ✓ Motor involvements
- ✓ Eye/hand coordination issues
- ✓ Executive dysfunction
- ✓ Language disorder
- ✓ Problems with content (confused details, events, names, etc.)
- ✓ Misuse of conventions (capitals, punctuation, etc.)
- ✓ Spelling difficulties
- ✓ Visual acuity, tracking and scanning problems
- ✓ Autism spectrum
- ✓ Narrative problems
- ✓ Disorder of working memory
- ✓ Short term or long term memory difficulties
- ✓ Challenges in dealing with concrete, abstract, or inferential information
- ✓ Self-checking or editing problems
- ✓ Association difficulties
- ✓ Sequencing difficulties
- ✓ Orthographic (writing) awareness challenges
- ✓ Phonological awareness challenges
- ✓ Time management issues
- ✓ Organization issues
- ✓ Confusion with idioms

✓ Variant or unsolidified learning style
✓ Variant relaxation styles
✓ Need for scaffolding and structure
✓ Diminished fund of knowledge

There are also a number of issues which are non-disability related. These include:

✓ Second language learners
✓ Disinterest
✓ Tiredness – lack of sleep
✓ Work/employment related difficulties
✓ Dehydration
✓ Diet/Nutrition
✓ Drugs and alcohol issues
✓ Poor environmental issues
✓ Ethics
✓ Family dysfunction and levels of support
✓ Socioeconomic factors
✓ Teacher knowledge of writing skill development (or lack thereof)

No wonder a "simple" writing disorder is so difficult to isolate. It is beyond the scope of this text to address all of these elements, but some time spent researching on the internet will yield a vast amount of information on any one of these topics. We will address a select few of them, however.

Dysgraphia is a specific learning disability that affects written expression. It is a processing disorder that involves motor and information in a developmental fashion. The demands of writing in schools change over time, so different skills are required. Some of the "soft signs" of dysgraphia include a tight, awkward pencil grip and body position, illegible handwriting, avoidance of writing or drawing tasks, getting tired when writing, and a multitude of written language difficulties.

Some psychological disorders are directly related to written expression. Graphophobia is a fear of writing or handwriting. Scriptophobia is a fear of writing in public. There is a website devoted fully to issues related to the fear of writing (www.fearofwriting.com).

One of the reasons why many people fear the act of writing may be due to their past experiences and how the topic was handled by adults. In an article entitled "No need to fear writing," Luci Scott tells the story of Elaine Maimon, Arizona State University West Provost, and her comments about how children are taught to write. If we use an approach that starts out by focusing on all the mistakes kids potentially could make, of course they will have no desire to proceed. From a very early time in our children's lives, we need to foster the belief that they are good writers, even if that effort starts with using drawn pictures to communicate. We need to stop pestering kids about every grammar error in their first draft. Instead, we need to encourage youngsters to get it down first, and then think about it, shape it, edit it, and finally produce a final copy. Ms. Maimon recommends that each student spend at least 10 minutes a day with paper and pencil or at a computer, writing something that will eventually be shown or published to someone else (Scott, 2004).

Some students experience real challenges in completing writing assignments due to an executive function disorder. They have difficulty planning, deciding on a direction or plan, organizing, using timelines, staying on task, detecting essential information and eliminating nonessential information, and self-monitoring of performance. An executive function disorder is often considered to be caused by damage to the frontal lobes of the brain (as well as some other areas). These students often have difficulty anticipating potential problems in their writing projects, and/or they are reluctant to take responsibility for such problems.

Children with an executive function disorder often have particular difficulty with free writing and unstructured journal writing tasks. What do I write about? For these students, it is often recommended to start with some warm-up activity and then provide a scaffolded or structured task that the students can work through in a step-by-step fashion. A great warm-up task involves a relaxation exercise with soft music, directions to slow down breathing, closing eyes, and imagining (or visualizing, or feeling yourself, or walking through, etc., depending on the learning styles of the students) being in a zoo, or a hot day, or boating down slow moving river, and other experiences. It can be a wonderful few minutes, an excellent way to start a writing class.

Working memory is an issue for many people with executive function problems. Working memory allows you to keep certain things in your immediate memory while doing something else. When you try to find the definition of a word in a dictionary, you must keep the word itself in mind as you leaf through the pages – your working memory allows you to do this. Some students may forget what they are writing about as they write – this may be a working memory issue. Dr. Mel Levine believes that writing may require more memory than any other skill in school (Levine, 2002). A wandering working memory can be a real issue for some students as they are writing lengthy essay responses to test questions. By the end of the composition, they forgot what the original question was, and their essay displays this fact.

There is an additional subgroup of youngsters, those who are challenged by Nonverbal Learning Disabilities (NLD), who also require specific interventions, support, and learning experiences. The key for these students is to facilitate their success at each task, helping them to gain positive experiences and to improve their confidence in their skills. Your author has long maintained that NLD is very much a "disorder of confidence." The writing approach we propose seems especially effective with this population.

In our own speech and language therapy sessions, we rarely work solely on one or two skills. Typically, a session includes work in five to seven areas because a number of skills are foundation skills for most language end products. The whole-brain approach to instruction makes the sessions go very quickly, and students rarely get bored or mentally overtaxed (after all, you are not stimulating the same part of the brain for too long…). We have developed activities for the following areas:

- Auditory and visual sequential memory
- Visual orientation

- Listening comprehension
- Reading comprehension
- Detecting the main idea
- Detecting supporting details
- Detecting the conclusion
- Following multistep directions
- Analogies
- Idioms
- Vocabulary (definition and context skills)
- Multiple meaning words
- Homonyms
- Word association/brainstorming
- Rapid automatic naming
- Grammar and language conventions
- Writing subskills in specific tasks (how to use quotation marks, for example)
- Word Forging® exercises with single sentence models, short essay prompts, and multiple paragraph assignments
- Specific speech skills if necessary (voice, articulation, fluency)
- Phonemic awareness and sound discrimination exercises if needed
- Social pragmatics skill development tasks

There are a number of neurodevelopmental functions which are important to writing. Good writers tend to have intact attention, memory, graphomotor, and higher order skills as well as appropriate language abilities. There can be problems, however, associated with each of these. For instance:

o Attention – distractibility, difficulty with task initiation, illegibility, numerous undetected errors, lack of effective organization
o Memory – word finding difficulty, organization problems
o Graphomotor – awkward pencil grip, difficult letter formation, malformed cursive handwriting, writing off the line or with poor margin control

o   Higher order skills – development of ideas, organization, making inferences, drawing conclusions, illogical argument, difficulty with essential and nonessential details, creativity, interpretation, evaluating, making predictions
o   Language – vocabulary, poor grammar, weak sentence structure, poor spelling, variant phrases or sentence sense

A disorder of written expression is usually not apparent at a very young age. Commonly, the first diagnosis is rarely made prior to first grade. There may be issues which come to the attention of the school staff, such as weak or no scribbling skills, poor tracing and copying, and difficulty in some specific drawing skills. A student may have difficulty with filling in blanks in pictures, words, or simple sentences.

Second grade is a time when more concrete signs of a writing deficit are potentially observed. However, issues related to the disorder of written expression are developmental. Some aspects of this disorder are not evident until the student reaches the middle grades, junior or senior high school, or even college – all dependent on the age-appropriate demands of the level. This is one reason why we cannot tolerate the contention that once a student has learned to write a decent sentence in third grade, he or she should not need any discrete instruction on sentence writing for the remainder of his or her educational career. Successful writing depends on the proper development of all of the prerequisite language skills at appropriate levels through high school and into college, including speaking, reading, organization, and others.

Evaluations should have more than just a grade level or a label (like ADD, LD, NLD, OCD, etc.). The best evaluations provide an accurate description of the student's strengths and weaknesses, along with perspectives about other factors which might be relevant to a judgment about how well a student is performing. Because the analysis of written expression is so complex and linked integrally with other academic skills, knowing an approximate grade level of performance can help to put the performance levels of a student into a perspective which parents can understand. A testing procedure that ends simply in "Johnnie is writing at a 7.2 grade level" is not sufficient, however, even if it seems to be what many people want.

The following are some standardized, normed tests which can provide some insight into a student's strengths and weaknesses:

The Written Expression Scale (WES) - [The Written Expression Scale, from the Oral and Written Language Scales, is designed to measure the ability to communicate meaningfully using written linguistic forms.] Writing skills are measured in the following three areas: Conventions (the ability to apply rules of spelling, capitalization, punctuation, etc.); Linguistics (the ability to use language forms such as modifiers, phrases, verb forms, complex sentences, etc.); and Content (the ability to communicate meaningfully through appropriate subject matter, coherence, word choice, etc.). The items, administered by age-appropriate item set rather than by basal and ceiling rules, provide a broad sample of writing performance. Ages 5.0 – 21.11. This is the assessment that we use most often. It is available from AGS Publishing, Circle Pines, MN. Its developer is Elizabeth Carrow-Wolfolk.

The Test of Written Language, 3rd edition – measures contrived writing including vocabulary, spelling, style (capitalization and punctuation), logical sentences (writing conceptually sound sentences), and sentence combining in specific subtests as well as spontaneous writing. Ages 7.6 – 17.11. We especially like the unstructured writing analysis of this assessment, although the scoring protocol penalizes a student for no or limited use of quotations, colons, questions, etc. which may not have been used in the story generated by the student. The Logical Sentences section may examine some elements which we have not often seen focused upon in high school instruction today. Developed by Hammill and Larsen, available at Pro Ed Publishers.

Other assessments include:

The Test of Early Written Language, 2nd edition – measures basic, global, and contextual writing. Ages 3 – 10.11. Available from Pearson Assessments, Bloomington, Minnesota.

Wechsler Individual Achievement Test II – a comprehensive assessment of academic skills, including spelling and written expression. Ages preK – 19+. The written expression section examines a student's writing skills at a variety of levels of language and his or her ability to develop ideas and details about a target topic. Organization, unity, coherence, vocabulary, and theme development are examined, as are sentence structure, word usage, grammar, punctuation, and capitalization. Available from the Psychological Corporation, San Antonio, Texas.

Woodcock-Johnson Pyschoeducational Battery, revised – includes dictation, proofing, writing fluency, and writing samples. Ages 5 – adult. There is also a new version, the W-J III Complete, that contains the Achievement Battery's writing subtests. Available from Riverside Publishing, Itasca, Illinois.

Steven Feifer and Philip Defina offer a comprehensive list of assessments which might be used to do a "90 Minute Dysgraphia Evaluation," including tests for intelligence, constructional dysgraphia, working memory, executive functions, writing and spelling, phonological awareness, retrieval fluency, and family history (Feifer and Defina, 2002).

Guidelines published by the American Speech-Language-Hearing Association's Ad Hoc Committee on Reading and Written Language Disorders (ASHA, 2001) note that assessment contexts and activities vary with the age and developmental level of the client being assessed. Here is a summary:

- Emergent level – family literary history, phonological awareness, print awareness, and spoken language
- Early elementary level – rapid naming, phonological memory, letter identification, invented spelling, reading, writing, and spoken language
- Later school level – reading, writing, curriculum-based language uses, metacognitive and executive functioning, and spoken language

(Note that the American Speech-Language-Hearing Association does not specifically recommend phonemic awareness assessment for high school students. There are other, more important and relevant issues to examine at that level. Many of the skills targeted in some of these assessments have not been specifically used by high school students for years, so they are often a little "rusty" – and a poor showing by an eleventh grader on a phonemic awareness screening does not mean he or she has dyslexia…)

We always combine a formal assessment (with comparison to normative data, standard scores, percentiles, etc.) with an informal assessment based on a free writing assignment (which we assess using the grade level analysis and a look at use of details, vocabulary, and descriptive adjectives and adverbs - the primary targets of the Word Forging® model). It is important to include functional writing samples in any assessment of a student's writing ability. Some students do very well in formal, structured evaluations, but their day-to-day writing in the classroom may be substantially less mature. Conversely, some norm-referenced and standardized testing is also recommended, as the inter-rater reliability of scoring free writing samples can be poor. This is another reason why we always use the grade-level analysis function of the word processor to determine the grade level of the student's informal composition – it removes the tester's subjectivity. In addition to a grade level, we also make recommendations for the positive effects that more details, more mature vocabulary, and use of descriptive language would have.

Here is a suggested format for assessing a more informal writing assessment:

1) Ask the student to write his/her name on a blank piece of paper.

2) Dictate grade appropriate sentences to the student (one can use Word Forging® methods to develop samples of sentences that would be grade or developmentally appropriate).

3) Ask the student to write a short paragraph about a school day, a favorite activity, a hobby, a sport, etc. – any topic of interest to the student. Prompt the student to include as many details as possible and to pretend the examiner knows nothing about the topic at all.

4) Record the start and stop time of the writing sample so that a rate (words per minute) can be calculated.

5) Make note if the student made an effort to proofread his or her own work and if any significant revisions were made in the essay based on this self-initiated review.

6) The assessor should evaluate and comment on the student's ability to perform the tasks (dictation and short essay) according to organization, sticking to the topic, penmanship, paragraph structure and development (topic sentence, details, conclusion) as well as correct use of grammar, sentence structure, spelling, and use of conventions (punctuation and capitalization).

7) The examiner should determine the grade level of the writing sample using a word processor's readability calculations. It may be necessary to correct minor spelling, grammar, and punctuation issues as well as correct sentence fragments before an accurate grade level can be determined. (Be sure to make note of this in any report.)

8) The school, school district, or state may recommend that a formal scoring rubric be used to evaluate the writing sample, for consistency's sake.

9) An inventory of any spelling, punctuation, and capitalization errors should be included in the assessment.

10) Some commentary should be made regarding the student's attitude toward writing. It is highly relevant if the student expresses attitudes such as a dislike for writing, a desire to

write as little as possible for any assignment, difficulty with major writing projects, a potential career in journalism, pride in a grade received for a written report, and other such statements. A confirmation of such an attitude should be obtained from interview of a parent or teacher who knows the student well.

A model for a comprehensive assessment rubric for writing skills is contained in Appendix D of this text.

We also examine student records, interview staff who work with the student, and look at past testing if available. It is additionally highly recommended to talk openly with the student regarding how he or she feels about writing skills. Some important insights can be gained. The student may overestimate skill levels or may have a very depressed level of self-confidence, sometimes one not based on reality.

The examiner may wish to look at the legibility of handwriting, particularly for younger students. The following is a list of parameters which might be relevant:

- ✓ Paper position
- ✓ Pencil grip
- ✓ Left/right handedness
- ✓ Formation of letters (lower case, upper case)
- ✓ Size of writing
- ✓ Spacing
- ✓ Slant
- ✓ Alignment on the line
- ✓ Speed of writing (short, timed samples can be obtained, similar to timed reading samples for oral decoding accuracy and rate)

Other aspects which the examiner may wish to observe and assess include fluency (the number of words written in a given time limit), T-unit length (the shortest grammatically correct segment that a passage can be divided into without creating fragments of a sentence), and idea density (the average number of discrete "ideas" expressed in each sentence).

There are many tests that will provide a grade level or standard score for a student's spelling performance. Some of these are quite involved, while others can be given and scored quite quickly. However, providing a grade level score or standard score does not necessarily tell us what we should focus on <u>tomorrow</u> in school interventions to help a student learn to spell better. We desire to have an assessment that will break down a student's performance into the varied encoding patterns and indicates where strengths, weaknesses, and likely targets for remediation exist. We recommend the following:

> **SPELL®** (Spelling Performance Evaluation for Language and Literacy®), by Julie Masterson, Kenn Apel, and Jan Wasowicz. This computerized assessment tool identifies weaknesses in spelling and recommends remediation plans. It determines why a student misspells and suggests specific types of word study to improve a student's spelling. The detailed and individualized report of learning objectives is very useful. Additional modules can assess a student's phoneme and syllable segmentation, phoneme discrimination, semantic relationship skills, and readiness for spelling words with prefixes and suffixes. It assesses consonant patterns, vowels, vowel + r, and vowel + l. The program also generates individual learning objectives for phonological awareness, alphabetic principle, letter-sound relationships, spelling rules, vocabulary, word parts and related prefixes and suffixes, base words, related words, and mental images of words.

One of the problems related to effective testing and diagnosis of a disorder of written expression is that there is a lack of consensus among many professionals as to which specific skills are required for success in schools. It is much easier to examine the skills for mechanics and use of conventions in written expression, but it is more difficult to determine the role of linguistic and cognitive skills involved in the process (Bradley-Johnson and Lesiak, 1989). Today, many states specify the target skills in their scoring rubrics for writing assessments.

When planning writing instruction programs or in evaluating the effectiveness of same, it is wise to assess often. We can give the students many opportunities to demonstrate their progress. Frequent assessments, however, preclude the use of normed tests because repeated exposure to a test may invalidate its findings.

We find great value in the use of a portfolio system of writing assessment and instruction. Portfolio assessment allows a view of the student's writing over time, involves the student in the process of assessment, usually has clear expectations, and promotes student responsibility in the process. It should be reasonable for the teachers of a given school grade to meet and reach some consensus about the writing skills that should be expected at that grade. Some states have produced guidelines, benchmarks, or frameworks by grade level for their teachers to use in the classroom.

The Commonwealth of Massachusetts, for example, has established frameworks for writing, consideration of audience and purpose, revising, Standard English conventions, organizing ideas in writing, research, and evaluating writing and presentations. Those same frameworks set out stages for various levels:

- Learning Standard # 19 – Writing – Students will write with a clear focus, coherent organization, and sufficient detail.
- Learning Standard #20 – Consideration of Audience and Purpose – Students will write for different audiences and purposes.
- Learning Standard #21 – Revising – Students will demonstrate improvement in organization, content, paragraph development, level of detail, style, tone, and word choice (diction) in their compositions after revising them.
- Learning Standard #22 – Standard English Conventions – Students will use knowledge of Standard English conventions in their writing, revising, and editing.
- Learning Standard #23 – Organizing Ideas in Writing –

Students will organize ideas in writing in a way that makes sense for their purpose.

- Learning Standard #24 – Research – Students will gather information from a variety of sources, analyze and evaluate the quality of the information they obtain, and use it to answer their own questions.

- Learning Standard #25 – Evaluating Writing and Presentations – Students will develop and use appropriate rhetorical, logical, and stylistic criteria for assessing final versions of their compositions or research projects before presenting them to varied audiences.

(Massachusetts English Language Arts
Curriculum Framework, June, 2001).

Wouldn't it be wonderful if a folder could follow each student, containing representative samples of the child's best independent work to meet these standards in written expression, each year in his or her school career? One of the most powerful tools we have employed in IEP and other school meetings has been a folder of the student's work. When a parent, advocate, or teacher claimed that a student could not possibly perform a certain writing skill, it was gratifying to pull out a sample of the student's work demonstrating that very skill. When a teacher can view an historical record of the student's progress in written expression skills, there is no need to try to discover at what level the student performs at the start of new school year in the next grade.

The portfolio could begin with such early written language steps as copies of the child's earliest scribbles. MacDonal (1997) highlighted various stages of early writing development: Stage 1 (2-3 year olds, random scribbling), Stage 2 (3 years, controlled scribbling, "writing" across the page in a linear fashion, repeated patterns), Stage 3 (3-4 years, letter-like formations), Stage 4 (4 years, letter and symbol relationships, writing one's name, copying some words), Stage 5 (4-5 years, invented spelling, grouping of letters to make a "word," copying small words from environment), and finally Stage 6 (5-7 years, standard spelling, formalized writing on a page). The portfolio could contain these early attempts at writing as well as other samples throughout the school career, culminating in the twelfth grade's major senior research paper and college application essay.

We need to do all that we can to facilitate the development of vocabulary skills in students. Shakespeare demonstrated a vocabulary of approximately 17,000 words in his literary works. Scholars figure that he added 3000 words and idioms to the English language. Children in elementary school are expected to know about 5000 words. High school graduates must know approximately 20,000 words, or more if they go into a very technical field.

Isaacson (1996) stated that there are two basic roles in writing: secretary (focusing on mechanical aspects of writing, spelling, punctuation, and handwriting), and author (formulates, organizes, and expresses ideas). A long-term portfolio of student work would be a comprehensive way to demonstrate the transition of a student from one role to the other.

If grade level targets are used, one may wish to know the general Flesch Readability Score details to aim for. Dubay, in work on readability scores (Dubay, 2004) details some guidelines. Flesch scores of 90-100 reflect "very easy reading" of sentences with 8 words or less, at the fourth grade level. "Standard" passages have a score of 60-70 with 21 words in sentences, at a seventh grade level. "Very difficult" reading has scores of 0-30, 29 words per sentence, at a college level of reading. Word processors which use the Flesch Reading Ease calculations will provide most of this information to the user.

We have never met a scoring rubric that completely met our needs. We consider it a bit presumptuous that we might delineate our own rubric that would meet all of our reader's needs, for every student at every level. Therefore, we have designed a model for a rubric that may be "tweakable" to the needs of your individual situation and student. A reasonable model for some Individual Education Plan (IEP) goals and objectives/benchmarks has been provided in Appendix C of this text. We will use that list to build our rubric, which is presented in Appendix D.

As an example, we might consider the case of "Mary," a

fifth grade student. Her IEP annual goal might read as follows:

After writing the first draft of a short essay, Mary will employ added information, more mature vocabulary, and descriptive language skills to expand the essay to an age-appropriate grade level in 90% of trials.

Benchmarks might include:

1) *Mary demonstrates the ability to use a dictionary, thesaurus, or synonym function for basic word selection tasks*
2) *Mary employs basic punctuation marks correctly (period, comma, colon, quotation marks, etc.)*
3) *Mary demonstrates the ability to employ macro-organization aspects (topic sentence, structured body with 3-5 details, sequential organization, and conclusion)*
4) *Mary develops an appropriate semantic map or graphic organizer to help organize writing*
5) *Mary composes sentences and short compositions at a developmentally appropriate level using Word Forging® techniques (increased details, mature vocabulary, added descriptive color) in handwritten and/or word processed compositions*

It will be up to the teacher to decide if Mary meets the benchmarks in her writing, but in order to meet the annual goal, her completed written samples (satisfying the benchmarks) will have to be at the fifth grade level.

X. WE WRITE WITH OUR BRAINS

Many skills and processes are involved in the act of putting ideas down on paper. It is crucially important, as part of the Word Forging® model, for parents, teachers, and even students themselves to understand some of these issues. Others (perhaps some of the aspects of anatomy and physiology) can best be left for another day of study. We have much to learn and assimilate about what will be useful in a practical way for our interventions for written expression, but let us not confuse the issue too much…

The learning style of a student is an important factor to consider. The basic learning styles familiar to most people include visual, auditory, tactile, and kinesthetic (movement). However, the multiple intelligences movement also tells us that people can also be "smart" or "not smart" in the musical/rhythmic, interpersonal, intrapersonal, naturalistic, and even common sense realms. Our experiences in the classroom and in hypnotherapy sessions tell us that if the student is not a visual learner, our attempt to have the person "visualize" some event or thing may meet with interference. If we ask our students how it felt to go to the amusement park, some of our auditory students may not relate to the question too well (we should ask them what they heard there). To combat the confusion that might be caused by these learning style preferences, we usually teach a lesson in the different types of learning styles and multiple intelligences, and thereafter our cues for writing tasks usually involve "imagining" the target item or event. In this manner, we tend not to confuse some students and let the individuals go in their own direction in terms of learning style. There are many learning style questionnaires available in texts and on the Internet. One that is particularly aimed at college students is on the website about accommodations of the Western New York Consortium of Disability Advocates (visit their valuable website at www.ccdanet.org/selfasses2.html). It encourages students to know what kind of assistance they may need at the college level.

A discussion of dominance in brain functions is needed at this point. Right-handed people tend, by a very large majority, to have a left-hemisphere language dominance. Some people are right-hemisphere dominant for language functions, and some people have a mixed dominance. In fact, the dominance location can switch, particularly if there is damage to the brain early in life. Left-brained people tend to be more verbal, analytic, deductive, abstract, concerned with the parts of a problem, linear or sequential in thought processes, and objective. Right-brained people tend to be more nonverbal, intuitive, holistic, sensuous, concrete, impulsive, subjective, and imaginative. Still other people are "balance-brained," which suggests that they use various processing skills based on the demand of the situation. Ideally, this would be a great way to go through life, picking and choosing the best path, but realistically, being balance-brained can cause some people to have difficulty. They get so caught up in the decision process of which skill or processing approach to use that the opportunity to act passes them by... People with "mixed" or "balance-brained" preferences may have trouble initiating tasks.

The skill of writing, unique to humans, is primarily a left hemisphere behavior in most people. Information is can be sensed as words in the occipital lobe (visual association) and the temporal lobe (auditory association). Wernicke's Area, in the temporal lobe, allows us to comprehend spoken or written language. Broca's Area, also in the frontal lobe, allows us to arrange sequences of words into sentences. It is often the experience of Speech and Language Pathologists that students who have difficulty with speech with also have difficulty with written expression.

Other areas of the brain which have potential impact on the skills of writing include various cortical areas, the angular gyrus (found between the auditory, visual and somatic areas of the brain, it has integrative functions important to reading and writing), supramarginal gyrus (important to abstract functions and word use), supplementary motor cortex (has functions for word finding and some speech production skills), and others. BUT – we are beginning to make this process far too complicated, so let's return to more practical aspects...

We used to believe that our brain processed information in a "linear" fashion. When we heard the word "pen," signals were sent from our ear to an auditory part of the brain, and then to Wernicke's Area and Broca's area so that motor parts of our brain could be stimulated, resulting in the muscles of our mouth moving so that our articulators formed the word "pen." This conceptualization of how the brain might work was based on past studies about the effects of damage to various parts of the brain. It was felt that different areas of the brain worked sequentially to help us adapt to our environment and to learn. Today, we know through the results of functional magnetic reflection imaging (fMRI) that the brain works more like a set of fireworks going off. It appears that a number of areas of the brain can be "lit up" simultaneously to facilitate processing of information.

A birth, most of the cortical neurons that we will ever have are present in our brain. The brain of the newborn is approximately one third the size of an adult brain. Connections (synapses) between brain cells (neurons) begin to develop based on our interaction with the environment. Connections that are valuable (used often) are maintained and strengthened through use. Those that are not used often are "pruned" off starting at age three years six months. The prefrontal areas of the brain, where integration of multiple association areas occurs, are the last to develop. Generally, our capacity to learn potentially is equal to the number of neurons plus the number of synapses. Myelinization (the production of a covering over the neurons) stabilizes and solidifies neural connections, similar to the "hard wiring" we have in a house. Changing the way a brain works is harder than getting it right the first time around.   This is one reason why slow, methodical, scaffolded learning may be better for some children than discovery learning, where one benefits from exploration and trial and error learning.

If the connections between brain cells are not used, they are pruned away – they die. The choice of which cells are retained and which are not retained depends on the demands of the environment. This kind of flexibility, or plasticity, has given us a distinct survival advantage. Childhood is a particularly crucial time for the "use it or lose it" process. Some skills, particularly some language and visual ones, have windows of opportunity known as "critical periods" that may close for good if those skills do not develop by the right age (Bragdon and Gamon, 2000).

There are many subskills and processes which support the ability to write effectively. These include:

o   Attention (previewing, self-monitoring, speed)
o   Expressive language
o   Receptive language
o   Memory (short term, long term, working memory)
o   Graphomotor
o   Organization
o   Creativity

Dr. Mel Levine, in his All Kinds of Minds website (www.allkindsofminds.org), provides in depth discussion of these and other elements.

To make a final connection for our readers between the ability to write well and the health and importance of our mind's functioning, we shall tell the results of the "Nun Study."

In 1991, some researchers began studying the cognitive health of 678 members of the School Sisters of Notre Dame congregation who were born before 1971. The nuns form a group with largely similar lifestyle variables, and several subsequent studies have looked at various subgroups within the entire nun pool to investigate possible correlations between the presence of old age dementia and other factors.

One such study (Snowdon, et al, 1996) looked at 93 participants who wrote short biographies when they first applied for membership in this religious order. The researchers looked at "idea density" and "grammatical complexity" of their application essays. The nuns who scored low in these respects in writing samples made early in their lives tended to develop Alzheimer's Disease in old age. Some nuns originally had written rather simple biographies, with simple, uncomplicated sentences. Others had composed biographies rich in detail, varied in sentence type and length, more colorful in descriptions, etc. The latter writing samples had a higher idea density. Idea density is considered the average number of ideas expressed in a set of words that is usually scaled to idea density per ten words. Ideas correspond to elementary propositions, typically verbs, adjectives, adverbs, or prepositional phrases, and relationships between ideas and propositions (Snowdon, et al, 1996).

Not a single nun who demonstrated high idea density evidenced Alzheimer's Disease when she got older.

Idea density can be calculated by the following steps:

1) Count the number of discrete ideas
2) Count the number of words in a sentence
3) Idea density = (the number of ideas divided by the number of words) x 10

Example: (The man went) (to the store) (to buy) (enough food) (for the party) (at his house) (tonight).

Density is (7 ideas/17 words) = 0.411 x 10 = 4.11

Low grammatical complexity reflects a simple, one-clause sentence with no embedding. Sentences with high grammatical complexity have several clauses, imbedded phrases, and more demands on the reader's working memory in order to process the information.

We are not implying that use of the Word Forging® process throughout your life will result in diminished likelihood that you will develop memory and dementia difficulties later in life. However, it is interesting that this approach reflects the findings of the "Nun Studies" in that more elaborate written expression in our early years could be a very positive sign in life. Which came first, poor writing skills or memory problems later in life, we will leave to others to determine.

XI. CHALLENGES TO REMEDIATION
OF WRITING DEFICITS

One of the biggest challenges to effective remediation of individual writing deficits is that we do not have a large amount of quality research into many topics related to the disorder of written expression. We can always use more definite data so that our methods are based on results.

Also, students today seem so stimulated in their own worlds that the traditional, and a one-modality approach to instruction does not seem to hold their attention for long. Anytime that a multitude of methods and motivators are used in effective instruction, it becomes more difficult to isolate the contributions of each parameter in research.

Another challenge that is commonly demonstrated in school programs is that the teachers in those programs sometimes have widely varying criteria for what they consider to be "good writing." Some teachers correct errors in their students' work; others do not. Some penalize for excessive errors; some do not. Some have been trained in the instruction of writing; some have not. It is difficult to establish statewide or national expectations for writing skills as the needs of different populations, different student groups, and different school programs differ so much. To establish some consistency, some states have established rubrics to use when evaluating written skills.

It is essential for school districts, however, also to establish district-wide expectations. If no guidelines or goals exist, one cannot expect any result other than a mosaic of expectations, desired competencies, and results. Staff training and development, mentor programs, administrative support, and funding are all parts of this process. If your school district has not made at least an attempt to implement a cohesive writing program from kindergarten through twelfth grade, ask why...

The process may include a system of accumulating anecdotal records (informal observations), protocols for student-teacher conferences, suggested contents of a writing portfolio, standards for grading of student papers, recommended checklists for criterion-referenced notations of student skill levels, and rubrics for assessment. See the next chapter in this book as well as the Word Forging® Companion for examples of some of these steps and items that a school district might consider employing.

A comment about the use of rubrics – some teachers do not like using them. They feel that students should obviously know or should already be aware of what an acceptable writing sample should contain. We find it just as obvious that these teachers are likely not aware of student preferences for right and left-brain instructional approaches. Some students like to discover and are intuitive; some students like all of the expectations laid out for them. A last thought – these same teachers are the ones who usually want to see, before a school year starts, all the expectations for which they will be assessed when it comes to annual staff performance evaluation time. Go figure!

It is not uncommon to find the desire to see a Special Education Teacher, Reading Teacher, or a Speech & Language Pathologist listed as the service provider for reading skill development in a high school student's IEP. Unfortunately, the service delivery grid often stipulates that "Reading" will be addressed in one, two, or three forty-five minute sessions a week. We have rarely seen the reading issues adequately addressed in this fashion, unless of course the decoding difficulties were due more to a lack of appropriate instruction, developmental immaturity, or emotional issues in the past. Just like in the younger grades, reading instruction at the high school or adult level needs to be performed in a consistent and regular fashion. Daily practice and learning opportunities are best. In fact, we would love to see in every document that a school district sends home to families a comment on the bottom of the page that states that success in school will be directly related to student effort, daily reading, and completion of homework on a consistent basis.

It has been our practice for a number of years to recommend specific computer software to our students who need support in oral decoding and spelling skills. Here are the titles:

- "Phonics Based Reading," © 2002 by Simply Media, Inc. It helps to build reading skills by teaching the sound components of words and the sound/symbol links in a systematic fashion. The program starts with short vowels and simple words, with hundreds of exercises. The student works and progresses at his or her own pace, moving on to more advanced levels once lower levers are mastered. There are three levels. The program automatically branches off to extra practice exercises in difficult areas as needed by the student. Displays give a representation of student progress with bar charts that can be printed and shared with teachers, etc. This is a great program to be used at home to support work done in school. The activities are varied and fun.

- "Phonics Based Reading for Adults," © 2002 by Simply Media, Inc. Like the "Reading" program above for younger students, this program is structured for success. Its activities, however, are at a higher level, including multisyllabic words and words with Anglo-Saxon, Latin, and Greek derivations. Practice in decoding, spelling, and using context to select words is provided. This program also has supplementary exercises if needed so that students can get extra practice in troublesome skills. It is a great resource for daily practice of essential reading skills in the privacy of your home. It also can print out bar charts to depict the user's progress.

We highly recommend these two pieces of software.

Some students may never reach a point where they can handwrite or word process well enough to meet their needs without additional supports. Yes, these students can use a scribe to whom they may dictate all of their work. Another alternative is to employ word prediction or speech synthesis software (MacArthur, 1998). These programs were originally designed for people with physical disabilities who could not manually handle a keyboard. In word prediction software, the student types the first few words of a word, and then the computer provides a drop-down list of alternatives from which to choose the right word. Speech synthesis software takes the spoken words of the student and transcribes them into typed words on the screen.

The National Commission on Writing, from the College Board, reported on four challenges that face us as we attempt to improve the writing skills of our nation:

- ✓ Time for writing (many skills are needed, skills cannot be taught in a few minutes here and a few minutes there, most children do not spend enough time practicing their writing skills, teachers are overloaded with demands on their time, having to read and correct the written work of many students each day overwhelms a teacher, many teachers just check to see if the assignment was done)
- ✓ Assessment and measuring results (fully assessing written work is a challenge, no single piece of writing by a student is sufficient to evaluate that student's writing skills in total, learning to write "right" needs to become a priority again)
- ✓ Integrating technology into the teaching and learning of writing (technology opens new opportunities for students to learn how to write and to learn the rules of grammar and composition, and the World Wide Web puts the world at the student's finger tips)
- ✓ Support for teaching and other classroom issues (funding for technology is needed, but also support for training is a priority; very few states require a course in writing for teacher certification)
(College Board, 2003)

The College Board (2003) commented that schools need to focus on the use of software to identify mistakes in spelling and grammar, the value of programs that permit students to share and edit their work together, the use of emerging programs to enhance the ability of students and teachers to assess writing samples, and the development of software to measure student writing compositions in a formal, standardized manner. Programs which employ the Word Forging® methodology will attempt to satisfy these requirements.

Additionally, many students (and many teachers) have no real clue about the power and capabilities of the word processing software which is available today. In workshop after workshop, we are astounded that teachers are not truly informed about how to change the settings for grammar checks (there are numerous options), format and set up options for printing, and other parameters. We have encountered some teachers who do not want to use the Word Forging® process because they tried it and found that the grammar check did not "catch" all the mistakes. (This was because the software's ability to find many common areas had been disabled or had never been properly set in the first place.) We know of one student who purposely "turned off" the major grammar checking abilities because he got tired of fixing the mistakes! We encourage educators and students to learn to use the power of the software which is at their fingertips.

XII. PRIORITY LIST FOR A
COMPREHENSIVE WRITING PROGRAM

If we were given the task of designing a comprehensive program for written expression within a school district or home school setting, the following would be ten primary features of that program:

1) In the early stages of school development, have students participate in writing tasks which are fun (seriously fun). Make sure such activities appeal to a variety of learning style preferences and right/left brained activities.

2) Establish a student writing portfolio set up with goals at each grade level, documented by assessment rubrics. If a given student fails to meet standard criteria set by the school district, then this information can be used to design an individualized remediatory set of lessons. A common set of rubrics, arranged by grade level, should be developed so that staff can become more consistent in their inter-rater evaluations.

3) Train all instructional staff in the basic expectations of written expression for each grade level, and include standards for adherence to expectations in the job performance evaluation process for such staff

4) Train staff in the method of a minimal marking approach to reviewing student writing samples, and enforce a consistent model of markings which facilitate the development of improved confidence in students

5) Establish a strong peer-editing program, including significant rewards for the contributions of the mentor students in the program

6) Encourage a model of vocabulary development which promotes use of context clues rather than depending on rote memory of weekly vocabulary lists

7) Have regularly held writing contests and milestones such as the completion of a major writing project at each major step of school (especially at the end of middle school, junior high, and the junior/senior year of high school)

8) If students with learning differences require added assistance to meet classroom expectations for written expression, they should work with a tutor or teacher to produce MORE samples of written work, not less; rather than focus on obscure or abstract writing skills, provide opportunities for students to learn the skills that will help them be more successful in school tomorrow

9) Require students to perform writing tasks often, encouraging the use of notes, comments, ideas, and assignments written in notebooks rather than dependence on short answer or multiple choice worksheets for assignments; have regular, meaningful checks of notebooks; make written expression a standard means of communication in the school environment, because it is the primary means of communication in many work settings

10) Instruct all students in the rationale and method of the Word Forging® process, starting in third grade, and weave the expectations of this process (learning to check one's own grade level of writing throughout the school years, and knowing how to get one's writing to the appropriate grade level) into the fabric of every school year until graduation – have the highest expectations!

11) Students preparing for college need to learn to be better self-advocates. They need to know where they need help and how to go about getting that assistance in college learning centers, writing centers, etc.

12) Provide students with *in depth* training in the use of their preferred word processor. (Many students, as well as teachers, are not aware of the various settings and capabilities of their software.)

XIII. INNOVATIVE AND RECOMMENDED ACTIVITIES FOR WRITING

Over the years, we have utilized a number of activities and learning tasks that easily support the Word Forging® model. What follows is a brief summary of some of them, followed by a list of recommended activities that are available commercially from other sources. We hope you find them useful.

A good rule of thumb to use when designing support activities is that you can never go wrong if you develop tasks that promote the student's use of his or her imagination. Idea generation is a key issue for many students.

To find a more comprehensive compilation of activities that fit well with this model of instruction, we recommend that you consult our <u>Word Forging® Companion,</u> a book of materials, worksheets, checklists, and activities that is available from Trek Associates.

<u>General Approach to Writing an Essay</u>

First, the student should plan his or her essay by selecting a topic. Generally, the student should organize thoughts and ideas on the topic and create an outline or graphic organizer to set them up in a logical manner in a pre-writing exercise. It may be useful to generate a list of key ideas or vocabulary that would be useful in the paper. Next, the student should start writing ideas into sentences on paper as a rough draft. Then the draft is edited for idea elaboration, spelling, punctuation, grammar, and language usage. This is when a computer's word processor comes in handy. Finally, the work is revised into a final draft. Here, it is helpful to put the essay aside for a day or two and then return to it for proofreading one last time.

Brainstorming

We usually think of brainstorming as a simple, "name as many items as you can in two minutes" drill. However, it is important to understand just how this process works. First, there are at least two brain processes, based on the part of the brain involved, of which all teachers should be aware. The right brain helps us be imaginative and innovative, and it assists our efforts to generate ideas. The left-brain tends to want us to organize things, to associate ideas closely into categories and groups. It wants to be a "gate keeper," deciding if something fits or not. Therefore, it is very important that the learner become adept at using both sides of the brain. Naturally, the individual may tend to be right-brained (very creative), left-brained (very structured and organized), or balance-brained (using the strengths of each side to help complete a given task based on its demands). Right-brained people tend to use visual associations; left-brained people tend to use verbal connections of ideas.

We have found the following simple activity to be useful as an ongoing learned skill for our students. Pick a broad category (at first, the teacher may select a category, but later it might be helpful to have the student pick "a category for which you know you can name a lot of things," instilling confidence just by the way we invite him or her to participate in the task). Examples can be "name things you might find in a store," "name things you see in a school," "name things related to summer," etc. The student is then given a time limit for naming as many items as s/he can. The time frame could be longer to start (one minute, two minutes), or it could be thirty seconds. We tend to use the thirty-second limit, and experience over the years has shown that most of our teenaged students should have as a goal 22 items named within 30 seconds. (Note: this goal is higher than norms on many standardized tests.) This may be a real challenge to start, and you may wish to adjust it down for younger students. It sounds optimistic, but once the student is shown the strategies of association (taking one idea and branching it into sub-groups or examples, and then moving on to the next idea), the score gradually goes up.

Having a concrete goal to work on ("Last week you were at 8 items/30 seconds, so today let's see if you can add to that…") helps considerably. It does not matter what the gain is from session to session; what matters is that there is general improvement over time. Some categories will be easier or more difficult than others (name things in this room, name occupations, name things related to sports, name things that have a lot of energy), but it is beneficial to challenge the students from time to time – just like exercising muscles in the gymnasium. It is important to maintain accurate data records, so you can demonstrate to the student his/her progress over time. Nothing breeds success like documented success: "When we started, you named only 9 items in thirty seconds – lately, you have been averaging 14 items!"

You will want to take note of the student's ability to use categories (if naming things in a house, does the student jump around – bed, knife, dog, basement – or employ some organization pattern – kitchen, silverware, knife, spoon, fork, plate, glasses, cups, dishwasher, soap?) and to avoid repeating previously named items.

This activity can be done with groups of students. A "round robin" format can be adapted so that the teacher goes from student to student, asking each to name another item associated to the target concept. If the student can name a new item, s/he stays in the game, until just one student remains. Another variation could be that students name items within their own category as the participants take turns (this may be useful with some students who can have some time to think of their next item, without the challenge of listening to others or having the dreaded experience of the item you have in mind being named by the student who went just before you). When all students work on the same category, it is necessary to establish the ground rule that no repetitions are allowed; this level of activity entails not only word association skills but also listening, attention, and memory skills.

A good source of ideas for brainstorming activities is James V. Smith, Jr.'s <u>Fiction Writer's Brainstormer</u>, published by Writer's Digest Books (Cincinnati, OH, 2000). Stuck with no ideas to write about? Consult this book for some great ideas to get the brain moving again…

Clustering

A useful pre-write strategy is to have the writer draw a circle in the center of a page in which the main topic is written. Lines are then drawn to smaller circles on the page. The writer attempts to fill in the smaller circles with ideas which related to the main idea. The process continues until new ideas are exhausted or a sufficient number of ideas have been generated. This is the conceptual mapping approach.

Forced Accuracy

We have used this technique in our visual and auditory memory work with students. Essentially, it involved asking a student to keep doing a task until he or she gets it correct. The same concept can be adapted for writing instruction. Tell the student explicitly what it is you want him or her to do (write a sentence with quotation marks, write a sentence that contains an adjective to describe each noun, write a twelve-word sentence). The student tries to do the task, and if the attempt is not correct, he or she tries again. The task is preceded by an explanation that the student need not hurry (if it takes all day, it is okay…). The point of the exercise is that the student _WILL_ succeed, and never again will he or she be able to say that s/he "cannot do it." Progress will never be made until that first, even faltering success is achieved. Then, in the next session, the aim is to do it again but a little faster, or do the task twice, or do it with no cues from the teacher, etc. We make it impossible for the student to feel failure, even if it takes some time.

Freewriting

The task of freewriting is when the writer composes some sentences or a short essay very quickly without judgment or in-depth thought. It is useful as a "warm up" activity, increasing fluency and strengthening right-brained activity. If one gets "stuck," the person should write the word "stuck" over and over until his/her brain kicks in a better response. The person should judge the brainstorming work; it is just a mental activity to get the juices flowing. These and other ideas about freewriting are offered by Sue Tomlinson (Tomlinson, 1998a).

Cueing

When your author has difficulty remembering the name of a person, he uses the alphabet to cue him for the person's first or last name. The technique is frequently effective. Other strategies include the use of the five senses, the five W's (who, what, when, where, why), a familiar sequence or map/layout, etc. The five W's format is so successful that we incorporate it into the first step of Word Forging®.

Time Capsule

This is a great idea. Ask all students to write a short statement, an essay, a poem, an autobiography, or a prediction that can be included in a time capsule. (The actual time capsule can be just a project which will not be buried in the ground, or it can be a real activity that will be put away for future generations to see.)

Journal Writing

Journal writing, regardless of whether or not the teacher grades the content, is a wonderful way to facilitate daily writing. The topics can be varied and interesting. The tasks can be just to brainstorm interesting responses, or they can be more structured as independent reading response booklets (read something and then answer a question about it). You can ask students to write about the following:
  ➤ An animal just like you
  ➤ Your obituary or epitaph
  ➤ The greatest event of the year
  ➤ The best skill you learned this year

- Summarize any topic in one sentence (pretend reader knows nothing)
- Your favorite set of clothes (and why)
- Your favorite show on television (and why)
- Your favorite type of music (and why)
- Your favorite meal (and why)
- A 100-year old tree has a ring in its trunk for each year it is alive. What do you think was going on in the world when that tree was 10 years old, 25 years old, 50 years old, and 100 years old?
- Describe your bedroom
- Write about the idea that excites you more than any other idea
- I have a dream…
- My biggest frustration
- Write a letter to someone you love
- Write a letter to someone you hate

Right/Left Brain Hands

Most of us (about 70% of the general population) are right-handed. Sue Tomlinson, in a series of websites devoted to the instruction of writing skills, provides a great activity for "Opposite Hand Exploration" (Tomlinson, 1998c). She suggests  that the learner attempt to do some free writing with the non-dominant hand. Research has shown that there is a fairly direct link between our non-dominant hand and our less verbal, more pictorial and pattern-conscious right brain. Tomlinson asks her student to establish a relaxed state and let the non-dominant hand write whatever it wants – "you will almost certainly be surprised." The topic may be child-like, reflect inner conflict (the adult, bossy left-brain arguing with the more creative, irresponsible right brain), but also create a fertile ground for creativity. Tomlinson notes that artists often attempt to spark creativity by spending a few minutes drawing with their non-dominant hand, sometimes evolving quite distinctive styles for each hand. Sometimes, in fact, the dominant and non-dominant hands can develop a conversation back and forth during free writing tasks, asking questions or making comments back and forth. Tomlinson's ideas are a great task to include in regular writing journals as an experimental journey into the inner workings of our minds. As she states, it does not matter if the reader can or can't make sense of these writings; what matters is that the writer get more in touch with the right brain. This is a case where the process (the activity) is infinitely more important than the product (the actual handwriting).

<u>Pruning</u>

Following Rawlins' advice for curing wordiness (Rawlins, 1996), students can be presented with a short paragraph. The goal is to have them work individually or in pairs as editors to trim (or prune) the excess so that a more effective sentence or passage is crafted. It is advised to start with a sentence, perhaps as an example, and then progress to longer paragraphs in repeated practice opportunities.

Consider this paragraph. Could you prune it to be more concise and efficient?

Let us first start with an initial step in the process of making a bed. You should begin by assembling all the needed pieces of the bedclothes, including top sheet, bottom sheet, pillowcase, and perhaps a blanket or comforter. Place these next to the bed. We think you will agree that having all of these materials close by will be helpful to you as you prepare to make the bed. Then, spread the bottom sheet across the bed and tightly fold each corner under the bed after you have spread and straightened the sheet over the mattress. Then repeat this process again with the top sheet, but leave the upper portion of the top sheet untucked. Likewise, place the blanket/comforter across the top of the bed and secure the lower portions of it by tucking them under the mattress. Finally, you can complete the process by placing the pillow into the pillowcase and subsequently laying it at the head of the bed. You then might want to tuck the blanket or comforter under the pillow or over top of the pillow, according to your preference.

Contests

Work alone or with a peer to craft the best sentence about... (fill in the blank). Have other students or teachers be judges. This can be a very enjoyable, yearly activity. You can also have contests throughout the year with different themes.

Writing Haiku Poems

Especially useful for practicing the skill of selecting vocabulary carefully and for learning to use descriptive words more vividly. Haiku poems have three lines, one with 5 syllables, the middle with 7, and the final line with five syllables. Here are some examples:

Greyhound
The world's fastest dog,
Quiet, sleeping on his bed –
A master's best friend.

Hypnosis
Soft, relaxed music,
Suggestive words, images,
The power of the mind.

Lake Home
Lakeside home at night...
The waves softly ebb and flow.
A full moon rises.

Haiku poems offer images or glimpses of life rather than complete comments. Teaching students to compose haiku poems helps to develop the concepts of word choice and selection of descriptive adjectives and adverbs. Some students become very adept at this type of composition.

Imagery Words

Ask students, in timed/untimed and individual/group tasks, to derive lists of words that assist in promoting imagery. For example, what words help us imagine the five senses (touch, smell, sight, hearing, taste), character descriptions, and other aspects? Here are some examples:

> Touch – hot, cold, slippery, velvety, rough, damp, hard
> Smell – perfumed, spicy, sour, fresh
> Sight – glossy, transparent, straight, narrow, immense
> Hearing – giggle, laugh, growl, whisper
> Taste – salty, sweet, tasteless, rotten
> Character traits – abusive, confident, dependable, generous, modest, patient, serious, thoughtful, wise

What words are related to various colors? Some might be turquoise, chrome, magenta, snowy, almond, cinnamon, strawberry, etc.

The Word Forging® Game

This is very simple, with materials available to most teachers and parents. All you need to do is have two dice. The students take turns rolling the dice. The player must compose a sentence using the number of words specified on the dice. If a total of seven is rolled, the boy or girl must make up a sentence with seven words in it. If a thirteen is rolled, he or she must devise a 13-word sentence. If two one's are rolled ("snake eyes," a total of two), the player loses his or her turn. Players take any specified number of turns (maybe seven or eight rounds), or the game can go on for a given amount of time (it makes a great "filler" activity after all of the formal classwork is done, until the bell rings). Scores are kept based on the cumulative number of words used in sentences by each player. The winner is the person who correctly used the most words in his or her sentences by the end of the game. A variation of the scoring would be to require players to make sentences of the length specified by their roll of the dice, and then they would accumulate points based on the grade level of their sentences (a sentence of 3.2 grade level would score 3.2 points). The winner would be the person with the highest point total after seven rounds of play. A variation of the scoring might be to do the activity on a computer. In his or her turn, the student needs to write a sentence using the number of words specified by the roll of the dice. Then, the grade level of the sentence is calculated. The player with the highest cumulative total of grade levels (6.2 + 5.7 + 3.4 = 15.3 total) is the winner.

This is a great activity to practice the basic components of Word Forging® in an oral rather than writing activity. It can also be done in the car or at home. It can highlight the fact that vocabulary is the key to mature sentences, not lots of words.

Foldable Word Forging® Activities

One activity that students appreciate is to fold a regular (8.5" x 11") piece of paper into a strip by folding it lengthwise five times. Then, fold it into a triangle and staple the base so that the form can stand alone. On each side of the triangle, write one of these words: details, vocabulary, adjectives/adverbs. The students can then decorate their Word Forging® triangle and keep it on their desk as a handy reminder of the elements of this method.

To help students organize their written compositions, you can also use a simple foldable graphic organizer. You can fold a piece of paper so that the result will help your students organize their next story or short essay. Dinah Zike has published a number of books (including The Big Books of Projects: Fast and Easy Projects for Everyone from Kindergarten through College, published by Dinah-Might Activities, Inc., 1995, ISBN 1882796039) that promote the use of "foldables" to help develop skills needed for English Language Arts, Math, Science, and other academic areas.

This format can be used for a single paragraph essay (with topic sentence, three details, and a concluding sentence) or a five paragraph essay (with introductory paragraph, three supporting paragraphs, and a concluding paragraph).

First, take a blank piece of paper and fold it into thirds as shown below.

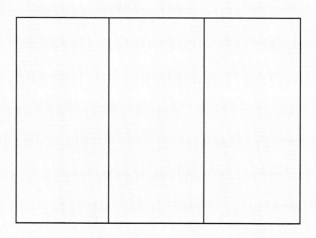

Next fold over the top of this page to about an inch. This fold-over section will now cover the top of your three columns.

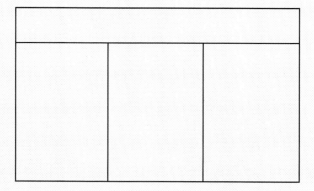

Take the lower corners of this page and fold them up so that they meet in the middle of the page.

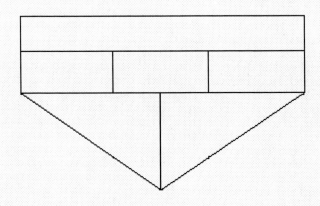

You now have a folding organizational manipulable to help organize compositions. Here is how it works.

On the top folded section, write the topic of the story, paragraph, or essay. Let's say the topic is "Breeds of Dogs."

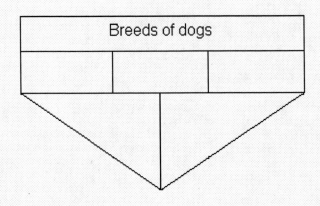

Then open up your folded paper and see the three columns again. Here will be recorded the three ideas or subtopics that will be used in support of the main topic of the paper.

Beagles	Collies	Dachsunds

In each of these columns, record your information that will be used to talk about each of these subtopics.

Beagles	Collies	Dachsunds
fdfkls fkldl kdfklsd dflkdfks kfdfkdlfslafk a fsfs ffsfa dfkldsdl dkfkdkdk ppodosasd	fdfkls fkldl kdfklsd dflkdfks kfdfkdlfslafk a fsfs ffsfa dfkldsdl dkfkdkdk ppodosasd	fdfkls fkldl kdfklsd dflkdfks kfdfkdlfslafk a fsfs ffsfa dfkldsdl dkfkdkdk ppodosasd

Now, there is a topic, the three supporting details (and comments for each), and now an introductory sentence (or paragraph) is required:

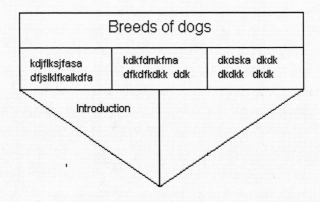

And finally the concluding sentence (or paragraph):

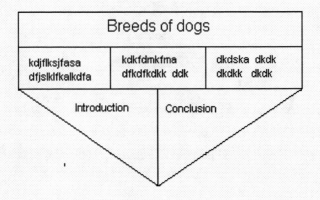

You now have a folding organizational tool that sets out your topic, three main points (and details to support each), your introduction (to get you "into" the information on the topic inside the folded paper) and your conclusion (to get you "out of" the information on the topic inside the folded paper).

For some students, having a manipulable which they use to visually and kinesthetically imagine their topic is a big help. Try it!

ADQ

We have sometimes observed teachers present comprehensive and length explanations of how students should respond to short answer reading comprehension questions. Many of these have been helpful to students. Some have been overwhelming; the students got lost in all of the options and alternatives. We sometimes have suggested that they employ the "ADQ" mnemonic… When responding, make sure they "A"nswer the question, provide "D"etails to support their answer, and include a "Q"uotation from the text. If they really want to score additional points, they can always add an "O"pinion about how well the issue being considered was handled in the text.

If you desire to look at other activities, worksheets, rubrics, and materials that fit well in the Word Forging® model, please feel free to consult the <u>Word Forging® Companion</u> which is available under separate cover.

Other Recommended Texts & Materials (in no particular order):

"EdHelper.com" – One of the best investments we made a few years ago was to subscribe to this website's offerings. There are worksheets and skill activities for a wide variety of academic areas, for young students as well as high schoolers. Rarely a week goes without our visiting the site and downloading an activity for our students to do, and they seem to enjoy the variety as well as the specificity of the lessons.

BarCharts, Inc.®, "English Composition and Style," June, 2002 – a

laminated "cheat sheet" type of basic guide highlighting key elements for the composition and editing of college level writing.,
SparkCharts™, "English Composition," ©2002 – similar to the Barcharts above, these laminated guide focus on essay writing, style guidelines, commonly confused words and phrases, a table of irregular verbs, commonly misspelled words, punctuation, sentence composition, paragraph composition, and essays.

The Daily Spark—180 easy to use lessons and class activities for Writing, by Nathan Barber, published by Spark Publishing. This book includes a multitude of great writing prompts that would facilitate a regimen of daily writing tasks that are interesting and fun to do. They make students think. For example, have your students pretend they are the substitute teacher for the day, or get the image of a sweltering day and write a paragraph using the words hot, humid, heat, or sun. It's a great book, one of a series of Spark books for academic skills.

Eats, Shoots, & Leaves, by Lynne Truss - This is a delightful book that, as the front cover states, offers a zero tolerance approach to the use of punctuation. Somewhat tongue in cheek but certainly with accuracy, the author provides example after example of how correct punctuation really does matter. The notations are humorous but will reinforce to the book's audience the importance of being careful while writing and proofreading. One example that has appeared on the internet to demonstrate Ms. Truss' wit is the following, from page seven (Truss, 2003):

> *A woman, without her man, is nothing.*
> *A woman: without her, man is nothing.*

There are a number of similar examples and anecdotes that could be read to a class full of students to provide increased awareness of how even small errors in punctuation use could have significant ramifications.

Craft Lessons: Teaching Writing K through 8, by Fletcher and Portalupi, published by Stenhouse Publishers. The authors maintain that we often focus on conceiving and correcting writing but pay too little attention to elements of voice, structure, supporting detail, setting, mood, and character. The book offers "craft lessons" which are fresh challenges and interesting tasks to facilitate the development of more in depth writing skills. The three sections of the book target primary students, grades 3-4, and middle school. The reasons for teaching an element, how to teach it, and resource material are included. This is a very useful text for a language arts teacher who wants to develop mini lessons (or use the text's lesson plans) for specific skills.

Inspiration® and Kidspiration™: Tools for Active Learning – Inspiration Software, Beaverton, OR – www.inspiration.com. Karen Franker offers "50 Uses of Inspiration® and Kidspiration™ which is very useful as an overview of the value of this program. Some uses include organizing information (for both students and teachers), plotting summaries, diagramming relationships, organizing one's notetaking, helping to study for a test, and others. See Ms. Franker's website at the following URL:
    http://www.uwstout.edu/soe/profdev/conceptmap/50uses.html

"Stack the Deck Writing Program," available from Stack the Deck Writing Program, PO Box 5253, Chicago, IL 60680, telephone: 800 253 5737. The core of this program is to teach four sentence manipulatory skills: combining, rearranging, subtracting, and expanding. It is felt that mastery of these skills not only improves a student's syntactic fluency but also provides him or her with a writer's vocabulary that will aid the student when s/he is revising a composition. Although this is a different approach to the composition of sentences, it reflects many of the elements we deemed necessary when Word Forging® was developed. Their website is at http://stackthedeck.com.

The Story Grammar Marker® Framework and Tool – This is a manipulative designed by Maryellen Moreau and Holly Fidrych to help children with comprehension and expression of the story grammar elements at the discourse level. It can be used to diagnose problems at the narrative level and to document and promote narrative growth. The approach also facilitates question generation, question answering, and story summarization. It can be very useful for some students to facilitate their use of graphic organizers and cohesive elements in narrative writing. More information can be found at the website of SGM Productions, Easthampton, MA (www.mindwingconcepts.com).

The Nuts and Bolts of College Writing, by Michael Harvey. This text, along with Nuts & Bolts: A practical guide to teaching college composition (Thomas Newkirk, editor), provides excellent insight into aspects of writing skills required at the college level.

The University of Calgary has produced an Alphabetical Index of Common Writing Errors on a website where the user can click on any number of common error types to see a description of that error. The website also includes links to other sites for information on structure, sentences, word usage, content, paragraphing, grammar, spelling, punctuation, and a marking guide index. The site is at: http://www.ucalgary.ca/UofC/eduweb/grammar/marking/alpha.htm

Writer's Inc. – A student handbook for Writing & Learning, by Patrick Sebranek, Verne Meyer, and Dave Kemper. It includes some great ideas and suggestions, including charts for transition words, linking words, various writing forms, terminology of writing, and writing topics.

The Write-Brain Workbook: 366 exercises to liberate your writing, by Bonnie Neubauer. This book is filled with varied exercises and writing tasks that will facilitate development of the creative side of one's writing. The goal is to complete one page a day. The activities are useful for both younger children as well as teenagers and adults. One never needs to be at a loss for ideas again.

"The Writer's Garden," a website by Mary L. Cash, that provides useful information on writing skills for a number of purposes. The website is at http://www.cyberlyber.com/kinds_or_writing.htm. The website also lists a directory of writing centers that appear on line, alphabetized. This directory is at the following URL:
            http://www.cyberlyber.com/writing_centers_list.htm.

Iacone, S. Write to the Point: How to Communicate in Business with Style and Purpose. New York: Barnes & Noble Books, 2003. "Fancy words and long-winded sentences do not make for successful writing. Rather, it's the skillful way we use words as tools to create and connect sentences."

Thinking Maps: A Common Visual Language for Learning, Teaching, and Leading, by David Hyerle.   Thinking Maps® have been implemented in schools with a focus on improving content learning and thinking. Students are increasingly overloaded with information, and the author presents a visual language (symbols) to improve thinking processes, communicating ideas and points of view, generating sustainable solutions, and assessing progress of programs, based on eight basic cognitive skills. The brain takes in information in visual, auditory, and kinesthetic ways, but the visual modality may be a primary means for many people.

"Quiddler," a spelling card game which my students enjoy playing. It is available from SET Enterprises, Inc., Fountain Hills, Arizona, or their website: www.setgame.com/quiddler.

Strunk, W. and White, E.B. The Elements of Style. New York: Longman Publishers, 2000. This text has long been considered one of the best resources for rules of usage and style in the English language.

Aaron, J.E. The Little, Brown Compact Handbook (5th edition). New York: Pearson Longman, 2004. This book has it all, including a section on how to use a computer effectively – except it does not contain insight in how to uses readability grade levels to help one improve writing skills. Otherwise, this is a GREAT holiday present for the person who wishes to get serious about writing.

Cliff's QuickReview – Writing: Grammar, Usage, and Style. This book is published by the people who produce Cliff's Notes (Wiley Publishing), and the book is written by Jean Eggenschwiler and Emily Dotson Biggs.

Warriner's English Grammar and Composition – actually written by John Warriner, Joseph Mersand, and Francis Griffith. Yes, this text is 40+ years old. It is very technical and comprehensive. Most copies of this book have worn covers and pen marks throughout the pages. This was the book that Mrs. Bishop had us use in my ninth grade English class. I don't know why, but I cannot just throw this one out.

Ross-Larson, B. Edit Yourself: A manual for everyone who works with words. New York: Barnes & Noble Books, 1996. This book includes a number of tips on how to trim the "fat" from your writing.

Adams, C.J. The Power to Write. New York: Barnes & Noble Books, 2003. This book includes a nice section on how to get the five senses involved in your writing.

Alward, E.C. and Alward, J.A. Punctuation Plain & Simple. New York: Barnes & Noble Books,   1997. Many common problem areas in punctuation are covered well in this text.

Andersen, R. <u>Powerful Writing Skills</u>. New York: Barnes & Noble Books, 1994. We love this quote from the book – "Nouns are where the information is. Adjectives are indispensable to speech, but there isn't one that can replace even the weakest noun." This is a very practical text for the person who wants to improve the style of his or her writing.

Shaw, H. <u>Errors in English and Ways to Correct Them</u>. New York: Barnes & Noble Books, 2005. The author attempts to dispel the misconception that writing is a complicated list of "do's" and "don'ts." He advises that you plan, revise, and proofread everything you write.

Sorenson, S. <u>Webster's New World Student Writing Handbook</u>. Foster City, CA: IDG Books Worldwide, Inc., 2000. This is a great resource for upper level students who wish to improve their performance on writing at the college level. Step by step instructions are provided, with examples.

Rozakis, L. <u>The Complete Idiot's Guide to Writing Well</u>. New York: Alpha Books, 2000. The author includes such things as ways to "cut your writing work in half by creating outlines you can really use."

DeVries, M.A. <u>The Business Writer's Book of Lists</u>. New York: Berkley Books, 1998. This text is full of lists (duh), all kinds of lists – including easy ways to arouse reader interest, proven strategies for overcoming writer's block, defamatory words that could get you in trouble, 200 prefixes and suffixes, and fighting words that could put your reader on the defensive.

Ehrenhaft, G. <u>Writing a Successful College Application Essay: The key to College Admission</u>. Hauppauge, NY: Barron's Educational Series, 1993. The text includes some wonderful, functional advice on how to write an effective college application essay.

Fields, V., Olson, J.A., Larson, V.L., and Godar, C. (2005). <u>Working Out with Writing</u>, available from Thinking Publications, Eau Claire, WI. This book has a number of writing exercises and tasks, all with prewriting, drafting, editing, revising, and evaluating aspects included.

<u>Writing Curriculum Week-By-Week Lessons</u> (Grade 1 and Grade 2), by

Kathleen Carden and Mary Godley-Sugrue, available from Scholastic (2005). These two books are a fantastic resource of weekly activities, with each task referenced by assignment, genre (expository, narrative, interview, persuasive, personal letter, etc.), skills targeted, and standards addressed. Simple rubrics which these young students can use to analyze their paragraphs or essays are included in the appendices.

The National Center for Learning Disabilities (NCLD), http://ld.org

All Kinds of Minds Website: http://www.allkindsofminds.org

Citation Machine – provides help with creating correct citations for MLA, APA, and other formats. You feed in the information, and the site formats the citation for you. http://citationmachine.net/index.php.

Lexicon of Learning – www.ascd.org – A list of terms used by educators so that one can understand the terminology

FYI - MicroSoft Word® has a feature that you can use to create automatically a summary of a paragraph or essay.
- AutoSummarize identifies the key points in a document. AutoSummarize works best on well-structured documents such as reports, articles, and scientific papers.
- Go to Tools, then select "AutoSummarize"
- Think of ways that this might help students in reading and text analysis!

XIV. CASE EXAMPLES

We have employed the Word Forging® methodology with a variety of ages and types of student. Students younger than third grade have been shown the approach, and they have become as excited about its use as our older students. Generally, however, we advise that the readability grade level calculations of the word processor be employed with students in third grade or above, as calculations below the third grade as not as useful to our approach.

We will provide some examples of how Word Forging® was utilized with individuals or in specific situations. Some people have asked if we get considerable improvements in grade level writing with all students, and some ask if the Word Forging® methods can be guaranteed to work. Suffice it to say that we have never had a student NOT improve the readability grade level of his or her writing if the steps and procedures of Word Forging® were used correctly. That same statement, a "guarantee" if you will, should be applicable to <u>any approach</u> for the instruction of written expression. (If it cannot be applicable, why are you using that approach?) So, we do not find the issue of a guarantee too bothersome or worth much attention.

We have employed this methodology with students in classrooms following a college-preparatory curriculum, in remediatory classroom settings with students who had learning differences, and in 1:1 tutorials with students who have been diagnosed with a written expression deficit. We have taught the Word Forging® triangle and the calculation of readability grade level in tenth grade English classes in Massachusetts where students were busily preparing for the written composition portion of the Massachusetts comprehensive tests, as well as to high school seniors who hoped to produce effective college application essays. Speech and Language Pathologists, School Psychologists, Reading Teachers, Resource Teachers, and Special Education Teachers have learned about Word Forging®. We have shown the method to people who work with school-aged and adult learners of English as a Second Language. We have instructed school teachers, parents, and administrators in the approach. Some of the people who saw demonstrations later told us that they demonstrated it to other students, parents, or teachers. It is because of input received from these people that we endeavored to record the Word Forging® philosophy and operational steps in this text.

One student got so excited about this approach to writing that he asked his parents to buy him a word processor. (He had avoided using a computer for schoolwork prior to this.)

Another student got very upset whenever she was asked to edit her own work. Once shown the rationale and methods of Word Forging®, she became very excited about the process of essay revision and fine-tuning, to the point where she professed that she would find the approach very useful in the career she was considering – journalism.

One young man hated writing, but once shown how to calculate his readability grade level and the simple steps he could employ to improve it, he would not stop writing until his sentences were at the twelfth grade level.

Once, when evaluating a teenager for a variety of language skills, your author described the Word Forging® techniques to the student. The boy's father had listened to the explanation, and while testing continued, the father went into the next room and proudly wrote an essay at a high school level – and then wrote another one for good measure. The clinician was sure that there would be no problem with adult role modeling of this new found skill in writing in that family.

Students learning English as a Second Language find the whole approach – using a computer to edit work easily, using spell and grammar checks, watching the grade level of one's work improve, etc. – facilitates the learning of the new language in all of its complexities. Students can work at their own pace, in class or at home.

Competitive students respond well to this approach. This is not so much because they can compete against other students, but because they can compete against themselves. A chart which the student can use to record progress is a very useful idea. Two months ago, she might have been averaging the 4.5 grade level in her essays. Today, she is at the 6.2 level, and only one year behind her goal.

School Speech and Language Pathologists, Resource Teachers, and School Psychologists have told us how easily they can employ the technique of calculating readability grade level in a free-write essay as an informative supplement to more standardized, normed written expression assessments as a measure of functional skills. It is interesting to see how some students score higher on the more structured tests while lower in a personal essay on a topic of their choice, and some students do the opposite – they write quite well in an original essay but may have difficulty with the targeted directions and tasks of a more standardized test. All of this is useful information to an examiner.

More than one set of parents told your author that their son or daughter had never been interested in writing home (or at least had never been very expressive in their letters or emails) until he or she started using the Word Forging® concepts. Communication was written more maturely, with more detail and description, than parents had seen before. In these cases, parents were eager to be shown "what you did to my child"…

School administrators are happy to hear that they do not have to go out and buy new technology for their classrooms in order to implement Word Forging®. The computers with the word processing software are already in the schools. Most administrators and teachers, however, are not aware of the "hidden" adjustments they can make to their software that will enable the readability grade level calculation ability.

Students enjoy being told exactly what they need to do to improve the level of their writing. Instead of hearing comments such as "make it better," "fix it," "write like a seventh grader," or "include more in your paragraphs," the students find value and utility in guidance such as "provide more details – pretend I know nothing about what you are writing – why was the boy running fast?" Others might be "combine two shorter sentences when possible to make the grade level higher," "use the computer's thesaurus or synonym feature to pick more mature words," or "liven it up a bit – use more describing words to make your sentences come alive!" For some students, the teacher or parent does not even have to give much direction. Once the student learns the basics of Word Forging®, his/her own experimentation and exploration will be a guide with two steps forward, one back, and two steps forward until the student reaches the level of writing that is desired.

Some teachers like the process because it puts the responsibility for finding many spelling, grammar, and usage errors on the student. They should learn to use the word processor's spell check and grammar check functions effectively, and a sort of "use it and learn" process happens. The more that the computer finds a specific error and prompts the student to fix it before proceeding any further, the more likely it is that the student will grow tired of having to fix that particular error and internalize the correct form in the future.

The thread that runs through much of these comments and experiences is that Word Forging® provides an element that is missing, misdirected, or difficult to establish in some of today's methodologies for the instruction of writing in schools – motivation. If you remember the basic tenets of our Triad Intervention[SM] philosophy, you will recognize the fact that many teachers or parents work to establish an appropriate goal as well as the specific instructional steps needed to reach the goal, but it is the bottom part of the triangle – achieving a sense of balance, need, motivation, or realization that work on this goal is like an idea whose time has come to the youngster's life – that is the most difficult to achieve. The fact that Word Forging® helps establish that foundation is the key to why it has so much potential.

Here is our final component of our demonstration of the Word Forging® model to you, our reader. Below, you will find a triangle. Without looking back through the text, fill in the three sides of the Word Forging® triangle. What are the three components of the model?

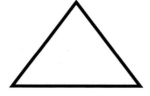

If you were successful, we trust Word Forging® will work for you.

XV. CONCLUSION

In writing this text, your author attempted to explain the Word Forging® process. The foundation of that model is based in the primary need to motivate learners to improve their writing skills. Without that fundamental achievement, the teacher or parent is continually fighting an uphill battle. We set out some basic requirements that our intervention for written expression improvement must meet, and Word Forging® satisfies them all.

At times in the previous pages, we also veered away from Word Forging® specifically in order to provide to our readers some historical, theoretical, and operational insights. We made the case for making the sentence the core element of all writing instruction. We beseech our readers not to be too focused on all of those details, however. (Worrying about so many details may not help you write better in class tomorrow.)

The Word Forging® approach itself, however, remains essentially simple:

1) Expand the number of details in your sentence. Accomplish this by answering questions (who, what, when, where, how, why) and/or combining shorter sentences into a longer sentence when appropriate
2) Increase the maturity of the word choices you make. When possible, use vocabulary words with more syllables or letters.
3) Add color to your writing by employing effective adjectives and adverbs.

At any step of writing from third grade and above, check the grade level of your writing often. This not only provides some guidance as to whether or not your improvements are working, but it provides immediate feedback as to whether the revisions and edits you are making do in fact improve your writing. This immediate feedback is an element that is missing from most traditional student-teacher models of writing instruction.

The use of word processors is highly recommended. This is due to three basic reasons: 1) the benefits of the computer's word processor for editing, revision, spelling checking, and grammar checking add much efficiency and power to the writing process when compared to the paper and pencil approach, 2) some students find writing with a word processor easier, especially students who have dysgraphia or handwriting issues, and 3) students will face challenges and demands in technology as they move into the work world of the 21st Century, and a lack of facility and competency in computer word processing may severely handicap them in the future.

Lyon (1996) details some important factors in successful writing programs. These include clear linkages between oral language, reading, and written language. The programs explicitly teach basic skill development in spelling and graphomotor production. These successful approaches teach students how to use strategies to guide the formulation of ideas for writing and the organization of these ideas on paper. The use of graphic organizers for prewriting, drafting, and publishing their work generally improves writing scores. Regular assessment of student progress relative to instructional goals results in higher achieving students in written expression. Intensity and explicitness of instruction are key elements.

Our experience tells us that many junior and senior high school students do far too little actual writing. The National Commission on Writing (College Board, 2003) reported that 97% of elementary students spent three hours or less each week on writing (this was the equivalent of 15% of the time the children spent watching television). It was also noted that 39% of high school students reported that they "never" or "hardly ever" were assigned papers of three or more pages per month. Then, the high school graduates hit a brick wall when they arrive at college or the corporate world where they are expected to do LOTS of writing.

Ovid, the ancient philosopher, is credited with saying the following words:

Gutta cavat lapidem.

This Latin phrase can be translated as "The water drop drills stone." This means that any act, even a simple drop of water, can have substantial results when it happens often enough. An indentation is formed, then a cavity, and then a hole grows as water repeatedly drops on that spot of the stone. Repetitive actions result in significant changes. So it is with writing skills. Practice makes perfect!

We feel that students who have more opportunities to write, especially if they employ the Word Forging® model, will become better writers. Put another way, it is our belief that "nothing makes a better writer than writing better." We should do all that we can to improve the writing fluency (rate and amount) that our children or students achieve on a regular basis.

One school administrator (to whom we demonstrated our Word Forging® methods) later sent us an email with the following message:

> *I wanted to let you know that the information you shared about your approach to writing has been so useful for my English as a Second Language classes. I have been working with our advanced students on developing their writing skills. The 'readability statistics' (which I NEVER knew about prior to talking to you) is a fantastic tool! The students have their own computers at home and are now checking the level of anything and everything they write. I believe they are actually writing a lot more, just for the fun of grading themselves. They have also found that your triangle is a great visual cue when they're composing written material. Thank you so, so much!*

We remind the reader of the simple effectiveness of our Triad Intervention^{SM} and Word Forging® principles. Make the act of writing improvement as simple as you can, and you will see positive results. It is when we make it too hard that students fail to learn.

We hope you will give Word Forging® a chance. Use it with your own writing samples before you work with students. Learn to see its value. Feel free to contact us with your ideas, questions, and results.

APPENDIX A:
Calculating Text Grade Level with a Word Processor

Microsoft® Word

Microsoft® Word can generate the Flesch Reading Ease score as well as the Flesch-Kincaid Grade level of a selected passage of text. A chart depicting an analysis of number of words, number of sentences, number of paragraphs, average number of sentences in a paragraph, average number of words in a sentence, average number of characters per words, and other parameters are included. You must run a spelling and grammar check before the scores will be generated.

To set up this software, you must follow these steps:

1) Go to Tools
2) Select Options
3) Select Spelling and Grammar
4) Select "Show readability statistics"
5) Run a Spelling & Grammar check from the Tools menu
6) At the conclusion of the check, scores will be generated

If you are unsure if your version of Word allows you to check readability levels, go to the HELP menu and search for instructions under the entry "readability."

You can run this scoring task on a full document or on an isolated sentence, paragraph, or section. Do this by selecting the desired text with your right mouse button, and then run a Spelling & Grammar check.

MicroSoft Word® has a feature that you can use to create automatically a summary of a paragraph or essay.
- AutoSummarize identifies the key points in a document. AutoSummarize works best on well-structured documents such as reports, articles, and scientific papers.
- Go to Tools, then select "AutoSummarize"
- Think of ways that this might help students in reading and text analysis!

Note: Reference to Microsoft® Word and its capability to generate text readability levels is made by permission of the Microsoft Corporation, One Microsoft Way, Redmond, WA 98052. Use of this reference implies no affiliation nor endorsement on the part of the Microsoft Corporation for the Word Forging® methodology.

Corel® WordPerfect®

Likewise, the Flesch-Kincaid Grade Level can be generated using Corel® WordPerfect® word processing software. To activate this process, follow these steps:

1) Go to the Tools menu
2) Select Grammatik
3) Select Options
4) Select Analysis
5) Select Readability
6) The Flesch-Kincaid Grade Level for the text is indicated by the first blue bar. A drop-down box allows the user to compare the open document to a Hemingway short story, the Gettysburg Address, and the instructions for 1040 EZ tax form instructions.

Note: Reference to Corel® WordPerfect® and its capability to generate text readability levels is made by permission of the Corel Corporation, 1600 Carling Avenue, Ottawa, Ontario, Canada K1Z 8R7. Use of this reference implies no affiliation nor endorsement on the part of the Corel Corporation for the Word Forging® methodology.

APPENDIX B:
THE WORD FORGING® MODEL

Word Forging®

Objective: The student will create sentences at an appropriate grade level by learning methods of increasing the complexity and length of his or her sentences.

"Word Forging®" refers to the use of *Microsoft® Word or Corel® WordPerfect®* to check the readability grade level as the student puts ideas in writing and then "tweaks" them, much as a literary author does. The model basically entails raising the grade level of written work by doing the following three steps:

1. Lengthen a sentence by adding words (either by combining shorter sentences into compound or complex sentences, or by adding information to the sentence by answering questions such as who, what, where, when, why and how?)
2. Raise vocabulary level (essentially, words with more syllables are often higher in grade level than simpler, one syllable words – "purchase" is better than "buy")
3. Add descriptive detail to the sentence by using more adjectives and adverbs

As the student works, s/he checks the grade level of the written work until it reaches the desired expectations. Sentences which use more mature, advanced vocabulary and have more words per sentence tend to be higher in grade level. Adding information, detail, descriptive words, and combining shorter sentences into compound or complex sentences are various methods to increase the grade level of written expression. The student should learn to manipulate these parameters and to check grade level/readability levels.

WORD FORGING®

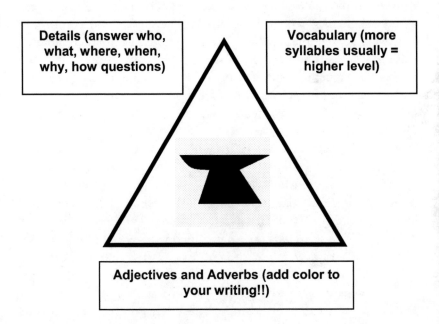

Details (answer who, what, where, when, why, how questions)

Vocabulary (more syllables usually = higher level)

Adjectives and Adverbs (add color to your writing!!)

APPENDIX C:
IEP GOALS & OBJECTIVES

The construction of truly effective Individual Education Plans for students who have learning challenges and diagnosed differences appears to be a rather difficult task for some professionals, especially for skills in the realm of written expression disabilities. We have seen a variety of goals, objectives, and benchmarks which have been generated. Our complaint, however, is that many of these have very little to do with the student's actual competence in writing tasks in school. They are either too vague, too specific, or too immeasurable. We prefer to create goals and objectives which are easily understood by parents, implementable by teachers, and sensible for students to understand.

IEP goals must be challenging to ensure that the student is held to a high standard. They must be measurable and should specify the expected knowledge, skill, behavior, or attitude to be achieved within the IEP period (usually one year). The goal should include evaluation strategies and/or criteria. The key to writing a good goal is to see it as a test that someone else could understand, implement, and evaluate at the end of the IEP period. The goal should be individualized. Objectives and benchmarks further clarify goals. An objective divides the skills within the annual goal into discrete, measurable components. Benchmarks describe the amount of progress a student is expected to make within a specific time segment of the IEP year. Benchmarks allow for regular checks of progress that coincide with progress report periods. It is not necessary to differentiate between objectives and benchmarks; it is important that each goal have objectives and/or benchmarks that indicate progress is being made or is not being made. Measurable goals are the key to identifying progress. (This summary of goals, objectives, and benchmarks is adapted from the IEP Progress Guide, April 2000, by the Massachusetts Department of Education.)

Here are some examples of some annual goals we might propose:

Given a basic simple sentence, X will employ added information, more mature vocabulary, and descriptive language skills to expand the sentence to an age-appropriate grade level in 90% of trials.

After writing the first draft of a short essay, X will employ added information, more mature vocabulary, and descriptive language skills to expand the essay to an age-appropriate grade level in 90% of trials.

Given a topic or idea, X will employ added information, more mature vocabulary, and descriptive language skills to compose 5 short essays at an age-appropriate grade level. (Met/Not Met)

Given a topic or idea, X will compose a rough draft of a major essay and then edit the draft using added information, vocabulary, and descriptive language skills in order to complete the essay at an age-appropriate grade level. (Met/Not Met)

Given instruction in specific strategies, the student will improve his/her written expression as demonstrated by completing 8/10 of specific writing benchmarks in the coming academic year.

As you can see, the goals are different according to the developmental level of the student. The first one or two are geared more toward elementary grade levels. The next two are focused on skills targeted in junior and senior high school. The last goal might work for any level.

The goals listed above represent end products of instruction in written expression. The day-to-day lessons will focus on the subskills and supporting abilities which will enable the student to achieve these goals. Therefore, benchmarks can be derived that are individually chosen based on the strengths and weaknesses of the individual student. The following is a list of subskills arranged essentially in developmental sequence from elementary to upper high school levels. When generating an IEP goal, the team can select the most appropriate goal (such as one of those above) and then chose objectives (such as those listed below) which can be developed into benchmarks.

The following is a compilation of written expression skills

organized according to general grade levels, although they are not exactly in chronological order as students develop differently. These could be employed as objectives or developed into benchmarks (by the end of the first quarter, the student will…) to target as a student works toward an annual goal. It would be appropriate to select two to five of the following in support of an annual goal:

Prekindergarten/Readiness
1) Student focuses visually on marks on a paper
2) Student scribbles with crayons
3) Student practices body movements such as up, down, left, right, forward and backward
4) Student practices making circles, lines, shapes, and large letter forms
5) Student completes dot-to-dot pictures
6) Student draws simplistic pictures of people and animals
7) Student engages in discussion about books or stories which have been read aloud by an adult
8) Student engages in pretend play about characters
9) Student role plays historical events or recent experiences
10) Student finds letters hidden in pictures to demonstrate visual discrimination skills
11) Student points to words in books
12) Student demonstrates that writing (pictures, letters, words) communicates different meanings or information
13) Student uses drawings to express thoughts, feelings or ideas
14) Student uses marks on paper to represent ideas and emotions
15) Student recognizes his or her own name on a card
16) Student recognizes familiar words in a book with increasing frequency
17) Student practices pretend writing
18) Student dictates short stories or poems

19) Student identifies key characters of a story

20) Student expresses feelings that might be felt by characters in a story

21) Student identifies the setting of a short story

22) Student identifies the key events of a short story

23) Student expresses how a short story ends (summary)

24) Student dictates simple sentences that demonstrate the ability to express a complete thought

25) Student demonstrates the ability to sequence events in story telling when presented on story board segments

26) Student arranges mixed-up events of a story in their correct order

27) Student writes own name on a paper, card, or sign-in sheet

28) Student uses writing materials (pencil, crayon, chalk, marker, paper, chalkboard, etc.) appropriately

29) Student demonstrates the ability to provide a basic ending to an unfinished story

Kindergarten to Second Grade

1) Student begins to use standard spellings

2) Student begins to use correct Standard English mechanics

3) Student demonstrates ability to identify the letters of his/her own name

4) Student demonstrates ability to copy his/her own name

5) Student demonstrates ability to write his/her own name

6) Student copies the alphabet letters and numbers 0-9

7) Student identifies letters in familiar words

8) Student copies familiar words

9) Student names the letters of the alphabet

10) Student writes the letters of the alphabet from memory

11) Student writes from left to right

12) Student employs simple sentences in written work

13) Student unscrambles words in a jumbled sentence to

create a meaningful sentence
14) Student writes basic declarative and interrogative sentences in writing
15) Student demonstrates basic sentence combining skills by joining two short sentences with the appropriate conjunction
16) Student demonstrates an understanding of the purpose of punctuation and knowledge of the basic types of punctuation
17) Student capitalizes the first word of a sentence, proper first and last names, months, titles (Mr., Mrs., Ms.)
18) Student puts a period at the end of a sentence
19) Student puts a question mark at the end of a question
20) Student begins to demonstrate the ability to employ the conjunction "and" to connect two shorter clauses or sentences into a longer sentence
21) Student puts a comma after a salutation, a closing, and between the day of month and the year in a date
22) Student uses commas to denote a series of words
23) Student uses pre-writing strategies to plan work
24) Student makes a rough draft of work
25) Student revises the rough draft for organization
26) Student is able to tell a cohesive story
27) Student is able to write a basic cohesive story
28) Student employs organizational structure (beginning, middle, end, sequence of events, etc.)
29) Student can create a basic semantic map
30) Student can create a basic outline of a story
31) Student demonstrates the ability to answer basic "wh" questions about a short story
32) Student edits work (spelling, grammar, punctuation, capitals)
33) Student incorporates support material (pictures, photos, etc.) into the work in preparation for publishing to an audience
34) Student employs appropriate margins in written work
35) Student uses appropriate spaces between words

36) Student composes a picture book
37) Student demonstrates the ability to draw a simple self portrait and to describe his/her basic characteristics in writing
38) Student composes a daily diary
39) Student can record daily work tasks in a work log
40) Student writes a friendly letter
41) Student composes a short story
42) Student composes a short poem
43) Student composes an invitation
44) Student composes a short narrative based on personal experience
45) Student summarizes a short story or book that was read
46) Student uses appropriate language for different audiences (parents, friends, teachers) and purposes
47) Student demonstrates the ability to use a basic graphic organizer to sort information into the appropriate category (might use picture cards that need to be organized)
48) Given a set of word flashcards, the student organizes the cards into basic sentences
49) Student composes a simple sentence at a developmentally appropriate level using Word Forging® techniques (increased details, mature vocabulary, added descriptive color) in handwritten and./or word processed compositions

Grades 3-5
1) Student creates exclamatory and imperative sentences in writing
2) Student uses correct noun-verb agreement
3) Student demonstrates knowledge of the basic parts of speech and how each is used
4) Student locates basic parts of speech in sentences
5) Student recognizes characteristics of nouns and uses adjectives to describe nouns in written work
6) Student uses adverbs in written work to describe

verbs and adjectives

7) Student demonstrates to use a dictionary for basic word selection tasks
8) Student recognizes active and passive voice
9) Student employs basic punctuation marks correctly (period, comma, colon, quotation marks, etc.)
10) Student puts a period after an abbreviation
11) Student employs an apostrophe in common contractions
12) Student employs an apostrophe to indicate possession
13) Student employs an exclamation point after words that make an exclamation
14) Student employs quotation marks before and after direct quotations
15) Student uses quotation marks for the title of an article, chapter of a book, and titles of poems and stories
16) Student underlines the title of a book
17) Student uses a colon in writing time
18) Student can employ basic forms of conjunctions (and, but, etc.) but avoids overuse of common conjunctions
19) Student avoids ending a sentence with a preposition
20) Student uses more advanced prewriting strategies (graphic organizers, semantic or story maps, webs, takes notes, brainstorms, organizes information based on the type of composition)
21) Student demonstrates the ability to employ macro-organization aspects (topic sentence, structured body with 3-5 details, sequential organization, and conclusion)
22) Student can develop a more extensive semantic map or graphic organizer to help organize writing
23) Student demonstrates the ability to employ micro-organization aspects (complete sentences, focus of thought, compound and complex sentence structures, and varied structure for maintaining the interest of the reader)
24) Student demonstrates ability to compose a rough

draft focusing on the development of a thesis, point of view, or description

25) Student employs effective drafting and editing strategies (idea elaboration, word selection, fine tuning according to the audience and purpose, production of multiple drafts)

26) Student revises his or her own work regarding details, vocabulary, and text structure

27) Student edits and publishes a written composition to improve use of grammar, punctuation, and spelling at a developmentally appropriate level, incorporating page format parameters (margins, indentations, etc.) and presentation material (pictures, charts, etc.)

28) Student gains facility in the use of a word processor with associated functions (spell check, grammar check, word count, grade level determination, etc.)

29) Student composes narrative essays (poems, stories, experiences, characters and plot, etc.)

30) Student composes expository essays (informational focus)

31) Student composes a short autobiography

32) Student composes opinion essays

33) Student composes essays of literary analysis (main idea, significant details, relation to personal experience, reference to other literature)

34) Student writes personal letters with all required components (date, address, greeting, body, closing, signature)

35) Student recognizes different audiences and writes a composition for specific audiences

36) Student demonstrates the ability to distinguish between fiction, nonfiction, dramatic literature, and poetry

37) Student identifies words or phrases that can be added to his or her writing to improve clarity or expression

38) Student can revise writing to add detail and images as well as combine sentences and rearrange text to vary sentences

39) Student composes sentences and short compositions at a developmentally appropriate level using Word Forging® techniques (increased details, mature vocabulary, added descriptive color) in handwritten and/or word processed compositions

Grades 6-8

1) Student uses compound sentences in writing
2) Student uses complex and compound-complex sentences in writing
3) Student uses coordinating conjunctions in written work
4) Student spells most words correctly in essays and compositions
5) Student uses colons, semi-colons, quotation marks, apostrophes in possessives, commas in phrases, and apostrophes in contractions in appropriate fashion
6) Student uses a colon to denote a list
7) Student uses effective prewriting strategies (outlines, more extensive use of background information, etc.)
8) Student employs a variety of sensory and figurative language in written compositions
9) Student employs a variety of perspectives in essays
10) Student employs effective editing, proofreading, and corrective strategies, focusing on clarity, word choice, and mature language usage
11) Student uses a word processor and associated software in an independent, efficient, and productive manner
12) Student demonstrates the ability to participate in appropriate peer editing tasks and to evaluate written work according to a rubric
13) Student writes a short story (situation, plot, characters, point of view, setting, conflict, resolution, etc.) with appropriate complexity, organization, and themes
14) Student demonstrates ability to use basic story elements (introduction, rising action, climax,

denouncement, resolution)

15) Student demonstrates ability to employ basic literary techniques (such as alliteration, rhyme scheme, simile, metaphor, personification, etc.)

16) Student writes biographical essays (including dialogue, physical description, background information, comparison to other people, significance to historical or personal perspectives)

17) Student composes a newspaper article

18) Student composes an essay to solve a problem (using clear identification of the issue and a logical solution)

19) Student composes an article predicting the future

20) Student creates a study guide in preparation for a content area class test

21) Student writes an analysis or response to a literary work (including impressions, inferences, and evaluative aspects)

22) Student composes business letters and letters of specific request

23) Student writes technical text (rules for an organization, lists of needed materials, rules of a game, etc.)

24) Student demonstrates the ability to edit written work for grammar, punctuation, capitalization, and spelling at an age appropriate level

25) Student composes sentences and short compositions at a developmentally appropriate level using Word Forging® techniques (increased details, mature vocabulary, added descriptive color) in handwritten and/or word processed compositions

Grades 9-12

1) Student independently uses a variety of organizational strategies and demonstrates the ability to select the most appropriate strategy for a given task

2) Student independently employs a variety of drafting and editing strategies (to rethink content, check accuracy of information, improve readability, address

needs of readers, ensure correctness of content and language)

3) Student independently uses a checklist for proofreading, grammar and punctuation, spelling, capitalization, and language at a developmentally appropriate level

4) Student demonstrates the ability to employ technology to publish his or her work (word processing, data processing, graphics, presentation, etc.)

5) Student demonstrates understanding of and ability to use various purposes for writing (explain, inform, analyze, entertain, reflect, persuade, etc.)

6) Student composes advanced grade-level expository essays

7) Student composes advanced grade-level fictional essays

8) Student composes advanced grade-level biographical and autobiographical essays

9) Student composes narrative stories with embedded episodes nested in one another

10) Student composes advanced grade-level observational essays (sequence of events, analysis, evaluation of importance, setting, supportive and descriptive detail, multisensory language, monologue and dialogue of characters, unifying theme, literary devices to enhance style and tone)

11) Student composes advanced grade-level persuasive essays

12) Student composes advanced grade-level reflective essays (using personal experience to provide perspective on life)

13) Student composes questions for research, develops a hypothesis and plan for research, and writes research reports

14) Student composes a well organized research paper that proves a thesis with logical organization, effective supporting detail, and variety in sentence structure

15) Student composes advanced grade-level responses to literature works which have been presented orally or through silent reading, including the author's style and use of literary devices

16) Student demonstrates the ability to use appropriate strategies to compose personal and business correspondence (informal letters, memos, job application letters, resumes, application letters, etc.)

17) Student demonstrates the ability to cite research sources appropriate in a paper or document

18) Student composes a college application essay at an appropriate grade level

19) Student demonstrates the ability to use different forms, styles, and tone when composing written samples for different audiences

20) Student creates a Microsoft® PowerPoint presentation on a topic of his or her choice

21) Student creates an informative website

22) Student demonstrates the ability to give a public speech using a written outline or index cards

23) Student demonstrates the ability to participate in a public debate, using effective research to support opinions

24) Given any topic, the student demonstrates the ability to generate a sentence that supports the underlying logic of the idea

25) Student composes sentences and short compositions at a developmentally appropriate level using Word Forging® techniques (increased details, mature vocabulary, added descriptive color) in handwritten and/or word processed compositions

APPENDIX D:
A COMPREHENSIVE
ASSESSMENT RUBRIC FOR WRITING SKILLS

Student: Date:
School: Teacher:
Grade: Class:

Scoring/Assessment:
   5 = Exceeds standard (advanced proficient)
   4 = Meets standard (proficient)
   3 = Basic competency (basic level proficiency)
   2 = Approaching standard (needs improvement)
   1 = Below standard (does not display the skill)
   0 = Not assessed/evaluated/applicable

ID #	Area	Skill	Score

TOTAL = _____

Comment:

The rubric blank is designed so that it can be used to address the developmental and academic needs of the students. The teacher would consult the list of subskills generated in Appendix C to fill in appropriate rubric targets. As the student masters skills, new rubrics are selected. It is important that students know what skills they are to be learning, practicing, and upon which they will be graded.

See the following page for an example of an actual rubric.

Student: *Jonathan Smith*　　　　　　Date: *June 20, 2006*
School: *American High School*　　　Teacher: *Mr. Dykstra*
Grade: *9*　　　　　　　　　　　　Class: *English*

Scoring/Assessment:
　　　5 = Exceeds standard (advanced proficient)
　　　4 = Meets standard (proficient)
　　　3 = Basic competency (basic level proficiency)
　　　2 = Approaching standard (needs improvement)
　　　1 = Below standard (does not display the skill)
　　　0 = Not assessed/evaluated/applicable

ID #	Area	Skill	Score
1	Essay composition	Composes a persuasive essay	4
2	Cites sources	Cites research sources appropriately	5
3	Proofreading	Independently uses a checklist for proofreading, grammar and punctuation, spelling, capitalization, and language at a developmentally appropriate level	3
4	Grade Level Check	Checks grade level to insure the essay is at the ninth grade level of readability; applies Word Forging® method to improve readability level as needed.	4
5	Public presentation	Gives a public speech using a written outline or index cards	4

TOTAL = _20/25_

Comment: *Jonathan, you composed a five-paragraph essay opposing the use of steroids in sports. It had an effective introduction and conclusion, but your essay would have been improved if you had included more supportive details. Organization was adequate. At times in your use of your word processor's spell check function, you chose an inappropriate word from the offered selections, making some of your sentences awkward. You did achieve a 9.4 grade level. Your oral presentation was appropriate, but you were a little nervous. Overall, good job, Jonathan!*

REFERENCES

Allen, R. (Summer, 2003). "Expanding Writing's Role in Learning: Teacher Training Holds Key to Change." Curriculum Update. Alexandria: Association for Supervision and Curriculum Development, pp. 1-8.

American Psychiatric Association. (1994). Diagnostic and Statistical Manual of Mental Disorders, fourth edition. Washington, D.C.

American Speech-Language-Hearing Association. (2001). Roles and responsibilities of speech-language pathologists with respect to reading and writing in children and adolescents (guidelines). Rockville, MD: Author.

Andersen, R. (1994). Powerful Writing Skills. New York: Barnes & Noble Books.

Barber, N. (2004). The Daily Spark—180 easy to use lessons and class activities for writing. New York: Spark Publishing.

Berry, R. (January/February 2006). "Beyond strategies: teacher beliefs and writing instruction in two primary inclusion classrooms," Journal of Learning Disabilities, 39:1, pp. 11-24.

Bradley-Johnson, S. and Lesiak, J.L. (1989). Problems in Written Expression: Assessment and Remediation. New York: The Guilford Press.

Bragdon, A.D. and Gamon, D. (2000). Use it or lose it! South Yarmouth, MA: Allen D. Bragdon Publishers.

The College Board. (April, 2003). "The Report of the National Commission on Writing - The Neglected R: The need for a Writing Revolution."

The College Board. (2005A). "Writing: A powerful message from
	state government." The National Commission on Writing
	for America's Families, Schools, and Colleges.

The College Board. (2005B). "Writing skills necessary for
	employment, says big business." The National
	Commission on Writing for America's Families, Schools,
	and Colleges. Retrieved June 28, 2006, from
	http://www.writingcommission.org/pr/writing_for_employ.
	html

Colorado State University. (2006). "Writing Guides –
	Introduction: Descriptive Detail." Retrieved June 28,
	2006, from http://writing.colostate.edu/guides/
	processes/detail

Corel® WordPerfect®, Corel Corporation, 1600 Carling Avenue,
	Ottawa, Ontario, Canada K1Z 8R7.

Cuban, M. (March 20, 2006). "What's Next Forum," Time
	Magazine, p. 90.

Devitt, J. (September 20, 2002). "Writing Program Continues
	Tradition of Innovation." Columbia News, Retrieved June
	28, 2006, from http://www.columbia.edu/cu/news/02
	/09/core_curriculum_writing.html

Dubay, W.H. (ed.). "The Price of Poor Writing." Retrieved June
	28, 2006, from http://www.impact-information.com/
	impactinfo/costs.htm

Dubay, W.H. (2004), "Principles of readability." Retrieved June
	28, 2006, from http://wwwimpact-information.com/
	impactinfo/readability02.pdf

Ehrenhaft, G. (1993). <u>Writing a Successful College Application Essay:</u>
   <u>The key to College Admission</u>. Hauppauge, NY: Barron's
   Educational Series.

Feifer, S.G. and Defina, P. A. (2002). "90 Minute Dysgraphia
   Evaluation." Retrieved June 28, 2006, from
   http://www.ldonline.org/ld_indepth/writing/
   dysgraphia_evaluation.html

Flesch, R. (1948). "A new readability yardstick." <u>Journal of</u>
   <u>Applied Psychology</u>. 32, pp. 221-233.

Fox News Network, LLC. (April 26, 2006). "Songbirds' grammar
   skills may revolutionize linguistics." Retrieved June 28,
   2006, from http://www.foxnews.com/
   0,3566,193232,00.html

Fry, E. (1968). "A readability formula that saves time." <u>Journal of</u>
   <u>Reading</u>, 11 (7), pp. 265-271.

Glazier, T. F. (1981). <u>The Least You Should Know About</u>
   <u>English: Basis Writing Skills.</u> New York: Holt, Rinehart,
   and Winston.

Gocsik, K. (2004). "Attending to Style." Retrieved June 28, 2006,
   from the Dartmouth College website,
   http://www.dartmouth.edu/~writing/materials/student/
   ac_paper/style.shtml

Gocsik, K. (2005). "Responding to student text," Retrieved June
   28, 2006, from the Dartmouth College website,
   http://www.dartmouth.edu/~writing/
   materials/faculty/methods/responding.html

Graham, S., and MacArthur, C. (1988). "Improving learning
   disabled students' skills at revising essays produced on a

word processor: Self-instructional strategy training. The Journal of Special Education, 22, pp. 133-152.

Graves, D. (1983). Writing: Teachers and Children at Work. Portsmouth, NH: Heinemann.

Gunning, R. (1952). The Technique of Clear Writing. New York: McGraw-Hill.

Hall, J.K. (1981). Evaluating and Improving Written Expression. Boston: Allyn & Bacon.

Hansen, J. (1987). When Writers Read. Portsmouth, NH: Heinemann.

Harvey, M. (2003). The Nuts and Bolts of College Writing. Indianapolis: Hackett Publishing Company, Inc.

Haswell, R. H. (1983). "Minimal Marking." College English 45, no. 6, pp. 166-170.

Harris, T.L. and Hodges, R.E. (eds.). (1995). The literary dictionary: The vocabulary of reading and writing. Newark, DE: International Reading Association.

Hyerle, D. (2006). Thinking Maps: A Common Visual Language for Learning, Teaching, and Leading. Cary, NC: Thinking Maps, Inc.

Isaacson, S. (1996). "Simple ways to assess the writing skills of students with learning disabilities," 1996, Retrieved June 28, 2006, from http://www.ldonline.org/ld_indepth/writing/isaacson_assessment.html

Jordan-Henley, J. (ed.). "Removing Word Clutter." Retrieved June 28, 2006, from http://www.rscc.cc.tn.us/owl&writingcenter/OWL/Clutter.html

Jorgensen, E. (2000). "A Night at the Bookstore." Retrieved June

28, 2006, from http://www.sff.net/people/
    ericj/backpage/1998/bookstor.htp

Kilborn, J. (2000). "Strategies for Reducing Wordiness." The Write
    Place, Retrieved June 28, 2006, from
    http://www.leo.stcloudstate.edu/style/wordiness.html

Levine, M., et al. (2006). The website for All Kinds of Minds.
    Retrieved June 28, 2006, from
    http://www.allkindsofminds.org

Levine, M. (2002). <u>A Mind at a Time</u>. New York: Simon &
    Schuster.

Levine, M., Reed, M., and Hapgood, A. (2000). "A Table of
    Neurodevelopmental Constructs." Chapel Hill, N.C.: The
    Clinical Center for the Study of Development and
    Learning at the University of North Carolina.

Lipkewich, A.E. (2001). "ABC's of the Writing Process –
    Editing." Retrieved June 28, 2006, from
    http://www.angelfire.com/wi/writingprocess/
    editing.html

Luttinger, H. J. and Gertner, M. (2005). "Learning Disorder:
    Written Expression." Retrieved May 20, 2005 from the
    eMedicine.com website,
    http://www.emedicine.com/ped/topic2801.html

Lyon, G.R. (1996) "Special Education for Students with Learning
    Disabilities: The future of children." Retrieved June 28,
    2006, from http://www.ldonline.org/ld_indepth/
    general_info/future_children.html

MacArthur, C.A. and Graham, S. (1987). "Learning disabled
    students' composing under three methods of text

production: Handwriting, word processing, and dictation."
The Journal of Special Education. 21 (3), pp. 22-42.

MacArthur, C.A., Graham, S., and Schwartz, S.S. (1993).
"Integrating word processing and strategy instruction into
a process approach to writing." School Psychology
Review. 22, pp. 671-681.

MacArthur, C.A. (1996). "Using technology to enhance the
writing processes of students with learning disabilities."
Journal of Learning Disabilities. 29:4, pp. 344-354.

MacArthur, C.A. (1998). "From illegible to understandable: how
word prediction and speech synthesis can help." Retrieved
June 28, 2006, from http://www.ldonline.org/
ld_indepth/technology/word_prediction.html

MacDonal, S. (1997). "The Portfolio and its use: a road map for
assessment." Southern Early Childhood website. Retrieved
June 28, 2006, from http://www.cem.msu.edu/~leej/
development-written.html

Massachusetts Department of Education. (2000). The IEP
Process Guide. Malden, MA: Mass. Dept. of Education.

McGinty, K. (ed.). "Nine Easy Steps to Longer Sentences."
Retrieved June 28, 2006, from
http://www.plainlanguage.gov/examples/humor/
9easysteps.cfm

Microsoft® Word, Microsoft Corporation, One Microsoft Way,
Redmond, WA 98052.

Moreau, M. and Fidrych, H. (1994, 1998) How to use the Story
Grammar Marker: A guide for improving speaking,
reading, and writing within your existing program.

Springfield, MA: MindWing Concepts, Inc. (website:
http://www.mindwingconcepts.com)

Neubauer, B. (2006). The Write-Brain Workbook. Cincinnati, OH:
Writer's Digest Books.

Newkirk, T. (editor). (1993). Nuts & Bolts: A practical guide to
teaching college composition. Portsmouth, NH:
Boynton/Cook Publishers, Inc.

Online Writing Lab at Purdue University. (2004). "Conciseness:
Methods of Eliminating Wordiness," 2004, Retrieved June
28, 2006, from http://owl.english.purdue.edu/
handouts/general/gl_concise.html

Pope, J. (2005). "Poor writing cost taxpayers $250 million a year."
Retrieved June 28, 2006, from
http://www.phillyburbs.com/pb~dyn/news/
1-07042005-510376.html

Porter, J.E., Noverr, D., Grabill, J. Swenson, J. and Wilson, M.
(2004). "Memorandum re: A plan for strengthening
undergraduate writing instruction." Retrieved June 28,
2006, from http://www.msu.edu/unit/provost/
inputs/AL07.html

Rawlins, J. (1992). The Writer's Way. Boston: Houghton Mifflin.
pp. 200-206.

Richards, R. (1999). "Writing and Dysgraphia," Retrieved June 28,
2006, from http://www.ldonline.org/article.php?max=
20&special_grouping=&id=550&loc=79

Ryan, C. (1996). "Business Communication: Successful Peer
Review." Fischer College of Business, Ohio State
University, Retrieved June 28, 2006, from

http://fisher.osu.edu/~ryan_3/resource/Peer.html

Scott, L. (2004). "No need to fear writing." Retrieved June 28, 2006, from http://azcentral.com/abgnews/ articles/0327maimon27.html

Simic, M. (1994). "Computer Assisted Writing Instruction." ERIC Clearinghouse on Reading, English, and Communication of the Indiana University School of Education, Digest #97, Retrieved June 28, 2006, from http://www.indiana.edu/~reading/ieo/digests/d97.html

Snowdon, D.A., et al. (1996). "Linguistic ability in early life and poor mental function and Alzheimer's Disease in late life." Journal of the American Medical Association. 275:7, pp. 528-532.

Stein, S. (1995). Stein on Writing. New York: St. Martin's Press.

Sweeney, L. (2002). "Information Explosion." Retrieved June 28, 2006, from http://privacy.cs.cmu.edu/people/ sweeney/explosion.html

Streur, C. (1999). "Creating prolific writers." Teaching Pre K-8, 30(1).

Thomas, C.C., Englert, C.S., and Gregg, S. (1987). "An analysis of errors and strategies in the expository writing of learning disabled students." Remedial and Special Education. 8, pp. 21-30.

Stringer, S. (1999). "Learning disabled students: Using process writing to build autonomy and self esteem." Journal of Instructional Psychology. September.

Tompkins, G. (2001) Literacy in the Twenty-First Century: A Balanced Approach. Second edition. Upper Saddle

River, NJ: Merrill Education.

Tomlinson, S. (1998A) "Free Writing." Retrieved June 28,
        2006, from http://www.delmar.edu/engl/instruct/
        stomlin/1301int/lessons/process/freewrit.htm

Tomlinson, S. (1998B). "The History of Writing," Retrieved
        June 28, 2006, from http://www.delmar.edu/engl/
        instruct/stomlin/1301int/lessons//language/history.htm

Tomlinson, S. (1998C). "Opposite Hand Exploration."   Retrieved
        June 28, 2006, from http://www.delmar.edu/
        engl/stomlin/1301int/lessons/process/nondom.htm

Tomlinson, S. (1998D). "Some Facts About Language."
        Retrieved June 28, 2006, from http://www.delmar.edu/
        engl/instruct/stomlin/1301int/lessons/language/
        language.htm

Truss, L. (2003). Eats, Shoots, & Leaves. New York: Gotham
        Books.

Uberuaga, B. (1993, updated 2005). "The Power of Information."
        Retrieved June 28, 2006, from http://www.buber.net/
        Blas/Writings/sh_print.html

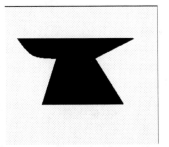

The Word Forging® Companion

We invite you to obtain a copy of this CD that offers actual worksheets, activity pages, charts, and other materials that can be used to support activities and methods described in the <u>Word Forging®</u> text. It is a valuable supplement for the parent or classroom teacher. The book format, stored in a PDF file, is designed to be easily printed and photocopied as needed.

Invitation for Online Word Forging® Certification

We also invite you to contact us for individualized consultation and coaching in the use of this methodology for your students or for yourself. The course is done by email, but telephone contact is also available to insure you understand and can use the techniques described in this book. *Certified WF Practitioners may purchase copies of the text at 50% discount, for personal use, resale, or training workshops.* For more information, send an email to WordForging@aol.com. There is a cost reduction for people who are recorded purchasers of the text.

Both of the opportunities above
are available from:

TREK ASSOCIATES
PO Box 110, Palmer, MA 01069
Tel/Fax: 413 283 6645
Email: TrekAssoc@aol.com
Website: http://www.wordforging.com

Steven Dykstra has worked with a variety of populations in Massachusetts since 1978, when he received his Master's Degree in Communication Disorders from the University of Rhode Island. He has been a Speech & Language Pathologist, teacher and tutor, administrator, and consultant to Early Intervention programs, public elementary and high schools, a private residential school for children with learning differences, a state residential program for developmentally disabled adults, a county house of corrections, and other settings. Steve has also taught several courses at the college level, on the topics of Language Development & Rehabilitation, Written Expression, and Counseling for Speech & Language Pathologists and Audiologists. He has conducted training workshops for professionals and parents. His expertise in testing and assessment has been considered valuable to many families and schools. In 1998, Steve culminated an interest in hypnosis and its potential uses in educational settings by becoming a certified hypnotherapist. His private practice, Trek Associates, features his skills as well as consulting professionals as needed. He has also done some computer programming for Microsoft© Windows applications for memory and language skills and has maintained his own website at http://www.wordforging.com.

Steve is available for workshops on Word Forging®, learning disabilities, speech and language development, nonverbal learning disabilities, academic focus & motivation, and related topics.

He lives with his wife and two children on Lake Thompson in Palmer, Massachusetts. Their greyhound dog, Joe, is a therapy dog certified by the MSPCA, currently in well-deserved retirement.

NOTES